KING DONALD

George Thomas Clark

ISBN: 978-1-7332981-0-0 – Trade Paperback
Copyright 2017 by George Thomas Clark

GeorgeThomasClark.com
Bakersfield, California
webmaster@GeorgeThomasClark.com

Books by George Thomas Clark

Paint it Blue
Hitler Here
The Bold Investor
Death in the Ring
Echoes from Saddam Hussein
Obama on Edge
Tales of Romance
In Other Hands
King Donald

Introduction

In King Donald readers join Donald Trump, Hillary Clinton, Bernie Sanders, Ted Cruz, Marco Rubio, Jeb Bush and many others on a raucous ride into a fictional world infused with facts from one of the roughest political races in modern U.S. history. Rubio rips The Donald who insults Megyn Kelly who counterattacks, and the candidates begin battling around the nation for months, and often reveal what they're thinking but dare not write. They don't have to. Author George Thomas Clark writes from their points of view, offering satire, humor, and pungent political analysis. Abraham Lincoln, Franklin Roosevelt, Vladimir Putin, and Benjamin Netanyahu also comment on the campaign.

Contents

ONE

1

Great Wall of Trump

I can't wait for the Republican primaries. I'll overwhelm the other candidates. I'm more celebrated than all combined. They aren't brilliant businessmen. They're bureaucrats who understand nothing but gobbling from the public trough. I showed them how a winner behaves, making a glorious escalator entrance into the audience at elegant Trump Tower and announcing my candidacy for president of the United States. The folks loved my speech, cheering and laughing in unison, and probably would have even if I hadn't paid them fifty bucks apiece.

They know I'm author of *The Art of the Deal* while Barack Obama is a Kenyan-born communist trying to destroy American supremacy by killing our economy. Don't believe propaganda about employment declining last month to less than six percent. Ladies and gentlemen, the rate's more like twenty-five percent, and most of those jobs are worthless. The good jobs we had are going to China and Mexico. They're beating us every day. They're beating a bunch of lazy politicians who don't understand the world. I'm an expert and really rich. Look at this official accounting. I'm worth around nine billion dollars, my cool name alone representing a third of that.

The Chinese and Mexicans already fear a Trump presidency. I may have to wait before I kick China's ass, but tomorrow I'm going to start building a Great Wall of Trump along our Mexican border, and I guarantee you the Mexicans will pay for it. I've already billed them fifty billion – dollars, not pesos – for fleets of trucks and bulldozers and armies of workers now headed for the treacherous border where very bad people daily enter our country. These aren't decent people, not more than a few, anyway. They're rapists and others with problems. Some are probably terrorists from the Middle East. How would we know? We'll soon find out. Here, look at the giant screens to see my artistic images of what the wall will soon look like. It'll be grander than the Great Wall of China, which we may also have to force the Chinese to build around their polluted nation of thieves and America bashers. Now, though, we're ready to seal off Mexico, and if Obama tries to stop my workers, I'll deport him to Nairobi. America needs a tough and economically skilled leader. I'm that guy.

Righteous Rick Santorum

I'm not surprised Donald Trump belly-flopped the moment he initiated his presidential campaign. The presidency is not for amateurs. We've already got a neophyte in the White House, and look at the horrific condition we're in. That will change when I become commander in chief. Unlike Trump and Barack Obama, I am no radical. I'm a thoughtful leader and student of history and therefore aware that from the 1880s to the 1920s we averaged about seven hundred fifty thousand legal immigrants a year. When I am president, we will simply lower the current figure of one million by twenty-five percent and begin to create a healthier nation. But we must remember that immigrants, be they legal or illegal, are coming in here and working for less than Americans and forcing wages down. This trend is more frightening than you may realize. There are fewer native Americans working now than in 2000, yet there are seventeen million more people in the workforce. Jeb Bush doesn't get it. That's why about illegal immigrants he says, "Yes, they broke the law, but it's not a felony. It's an act of love, it's an act of commitment to your family."

While Jeb and The Donald dirty themselves, I'm going to say something we all surely agree on: "If these ISIS folks want to return to a seventh century version of Islam, then let's load up our bombers and bomb them back to the seventh century... Radical Islam is confronting this country. Terror is a tactic, and radical Islam is an ideology." It is a threat President Santorum will rapidly crush.

You can be confident I know how to protect innocent lives. For that reason I would never attend a gay wedding. Such immoral and unnatural unions cannot result in the conception of children, and all adoptive children thrust into that environment would likely develop perverse values. We must also protect our young by overturning Roe v. Wade, murderous legislation I believe a majority of Americans despise. We need many happy and healthy children, and President Santorum will ensure their good health by also overturning Obamacare, which has gutted the nation's health care system.

Those of you who know me know I can win. The many who still, distressingly, haven't heard the name Rick Santorum should understand that in 2012 I won primaries in Iowa, Colorado, Minnesota, and Missouri, and came within a whisker elsewhere despite not having the money of presumptuous frontrunner Mitt Romney. Campaign 2016 is going to be different. My website is designed to make it easy for you to contribute. Donate something for rational immigration policies and against ISIS, gay marriage, abortions, and Obamacare. Let's make America great again.

Bold Rubio Spanks Trump

It's unfair that liberal opponents of my presidential campaign, which is becoming a juggernaut, are criticizing me, and also other Republicans but mostly me, for waiting two weeks before denouncing Donald Trump for his remarks that most Mexicans who enter the United States are criminals and rapists and not the best people. Please understand, I would've instantly denounced The Donald had he been referring to brave Cubans who risk their lives to come here in small boats to escape the criminal Castro brothers. This is blood and politics, and in Florida many of my wealthiest and most powerful supporters are, like me, of Cuban ancestry.

I love Mexicans and assure you I love them more than Donald Trump and all of the countless other Republican candidates. I can best help law-abiding Mexicans by becoming president and I'm more likely to do so by saying nothing even when saying something is called for but politically dangerous. What if I'd denounced Trump and suffered a conservative backlash. Okay, once I'd carefully determined that the majority of the electorate, and many companies, and millions of Mexicans, and even other Republican candidates like Governor Rick Perry of Texas and former Governor George Pataki of New York had said, at minimum, that Trump was out of line, I stepped up and stated that his "comments are not just offensive and inaccurate, but also divisive. Our next president needs to be someone who brings Americans together – not someone who continues to divide."

What really outrages me and spurs me to speak immediately are moves by the Obama administration to normalize relations with Cuba. I would prefer another fifty-five years of tension and failed attempts to isolate the communists and perhaps at least one more Cuban Missile Crisis. I'd be prompt and presidential then, and that's what America needs.

More Great Walls of Trump

I'm glad people challenged my remarks that illegal Mexicans entering the United States are rapists. They spurred me to do more research and review the article I'd read in Fusion, which is owned by hypocritical Univision, and I found something far worse than I'd asserted in my original statements. You may not want to believe, but must since the sources are unimpeachably Hispanic, that eighty percent of Central American girls and women who try to travel through Mexico to the United States are raped. That's appalling.

You know Barack Obama won't do anything. That's why I've already started rapidly building my Great Wall of Trump on our southern border with Mexico. Now, as a humanitarian as well as patriot, I will soon also send my armies of engineers, workers, and equipment to Mexico's southern border with Guatemala and Central America to seal off the godforsaken Mexican territory so more innocent women won't enter and be raped or murdered.

Someone must do this, and I'm the only one brave, talented, and rich enough to get the job done. Let's be honest: there are currently three hundred thousand illegal Mexicans in our state and federal jails. We must send them home. America can never be home to countless new criminals. We do have quite a few homegrown wretches we can't comfortably accommodate and really should send them to my new walled Mexico. Listen, I love the Mexican people, and most of those I've met love me. But they're killing us at the border and taking our jobs, manufacturing, and money. That's not entirely their fault. Their leaders are smarter than ours and will be until I'm elected president. In the meantime, in about two minutes, I'm sending another construction crew to build an impenetrable wall around the White House so Obama can't get out and squander any more of our national wealth and dignity. If the president tries to circumvent my orders, I may have to electrify that wall, and cyber-jam and otherwise quarantine his residence, keeping him incommunicado and under house arrest, until I'm ready to move in.

TWO

Hillary's Emails

I hope you already know that attacks on me for having a private email server while secretary of state are nothing more than a continuance of the vast right-wing conspiracy against Bill and me and have nothing to do with national security or legality or even ethics. It's all about politics and the determination of fascist elements to prevent me from becoming president of the United States. We all know I should have won the election in 2008. Barack Obama was inexperienced and weak on foreign policy but excited millions with rather hollow oratory and the stunning prospect of becoming the first black president. Trust me, if Obama's white, I win the election.

President Obama, trapped in the Republican-induced economic catastrophe, also knew I'd likely challenge and defeat him in the 2012 Democratic primary if he didn't somehow neutralize me. That he did by appointing me secretary of state. Then he and his agents planned to keep me under surveillance and read my emails. Fanatical conservatives also wanted to snoop, but I didn't let them. I established my own secure server for personal emails, and that was my right and my duty.

I never knowingly sent any classified information through my private server. I thought I was using the State Department's when I emailed or received information about the attack on our embassy in Benghazi and that Ambassador Chris Stevens was there, and I typed a few details about NATO bombing plans in Libya. This was a tense and tragic time. It doesn't matter which server I used. I was forging U.S. foreign policy while we were under attack. Now I'm assailed for being a patriot and fighting our enemies. That's got to be political.

Attempts to block my rightful path to the presidency simply will not work. I've already given investigators more than thirty thousand emails and am tired of their complaints the messages are "heavily redacted." This precaution is essential to protect national dignity. Additionally, my staff has deleted thirty-one thousand emails that were assuredly personal and, prudently, turned my server over to the government. I bet you have different servers for home and work. Settle down, and read two examples of my always appropriate emails.

To _____,

Vladimir _____ just sent me a wonderful recipe for chocolate chip cookies. He knows he'll soon be dealing with me and wants to build a positive relationship that's been impossible with a radical like President _____. Some advisers have said, "Be careful. He doesn't want to negotiate with you after 2016 and is trying to fatten you up so you lose either in the primaries or general election." I doubt that. He's a thoughtful man who knows I love baking cookies and am disciplined enough to make sure my _____ doesn't get any fatter. True, I'm not likely to ever be thin again, but Bubba's no ballerina, either. I expect conservatives to say or imply it's all right for a male politician to be obese, like _____ Christie, but that a woman who's merely chubby should be rejected. Voters are now too sophisticated to tolerate such hypocrisy. Look at _____ Palin and _____ Bachmann. They're hard-bodied but crazy as _____, and we know what voters decided about them.

Hillary

To _____ and _____,

Please keep your eyes on Bill when I'm meeting foreign leaders overseas. I know you've said we couldn't even keep track of him when he was right down the White House hall with Monica _____. It's more important now. Bill was already president. I still have to win the elections. I can't do that if my husband creates more scandals. I know he can't say no when he has opportunities, so I want you and others we trust to make sure he doesn't get many good openings. If he ruins my chance to become president, I'm afraid I might cut his _____ off.

Hillary

Kasich Must Gamble

(This memo to Ohio Governor John Kasich from his top political adviser was leaked early this morning.)

I am not going to send you falsely optimistic analyses of your prospects in the Republican presidential primary. I'm going to tell the truth. It doesn't matter that you were the youngest man ever elected to the Ohio Senate or that you served nine terms in the U.S. House of Representatives and chaired the House Budget Committee and in 1997 were hailed "chief architect of a deal that balanced the federal budget for the first time since 1969" or that you have twice been elected governor of Ohio and can tout some success in jobs creation and budget control. Those things don't matter much when you're running for the presidency, and neither does it that you initially failed to appoint a single person of color to your gubernatorial cabinet and told a plaintive black state senator, "I don't need your people."

Stances on issues don't count much as long as a candidate isn't perceived as a crackpot. What counts is who looks and sounds cool, like Obama and W and Bubba and Reagan. Those guys get the girls as well as plenty of votes from men. I'm not suggesting you're a klutz, Governor, but you're a rather dreary supporting actor competing for the hottest lead role in the world. Don't forget, you first tried to become president in 1999, forming an exploratory committee, but couldn't raise more than chickenfeed and dropped out to support charming blowhard George W. Bush. You probably felt like those poor guys years earlier who'd heard the bedroom door shut after W escorted the prettiest cheerleader down the hallway.

Before the first debate I wasn't sure who should be favored to win the Republican primary. Now I understand Senator Marco Rubio is the real frontrunner. In the TV era, now amplified by YouTube, the most personally popular candidate has prevailed: JFK v. Nixon, Reagan v. Carter, Bubba v. Poppa Bush, W v. Gore and Kerry, Obama v. McCain and Romney. Marco Rubio's a leading man like the five aforementioned winners. Most women aren't going to vote against a young, good looking guy. He's also bright and articulate. Really, he's about got the nomination sealed unless you do something transformational. Don't bother petulantly attacking him during debates. Accept that he's going to surge. And roll the dice.

Here's what you must do. Arrange a secret meeting with President Obama. Admit the political realities I've delineated above. And promise him if you become president you'll protect and expand Obamacare and support the nuclear treaty with Iran. Those are the right moves for the nation and world but you obviously can't admit that during the campaign. Obama will want to know what you expect in return. Tell him you need his ultimate limousine, The Beast. I think he'll say yes. He's rumored to have a dozen, and can get by with eleven.

You need to start appearing at all political events in your Kasich Beast, nearly ten tons of steel and toughness boasting blast and bulletproof windows five inches thick and doors eight inches wide and heavy as doors on large passenger jets. You need a limo eighteen feet long that can be sealed during a biochemical attack and is equipped with tear gas cannons and night vision cameras in front and a steel protector five inches thick underneath and puncture-resistant tires capable of rolling on steel rims and a satellite phone connected to everyone essential. Get one of those babies and you'll rise in the polls, guaranteed. But I can't guarantee that having the baddest car will make you the most popular cat. Nor can I promise that President Obama will make this deal. Convince him that his foreign and domestic legacies will be dismantled by anyone but President Kasich. You'll also need to persuade him that Hillary Clinton can't win.

Megyn Kelly Counterattacks

I was professional and dignified during the first Republican presidential debate as well as afterward, but now, on my day off, I'm tired of being restrained about Donald Trump, who I questioned about his many insulting remarks regarding the appearance of women who displeased him. He enjoys calling them "fat pigs, dogs, slobs, and disgusting animals." Do we really want a president so crude and condescending? We decidedly do not. Mr. Trump wasn't satisfied merely rebuking me for not being nice to him, which he claims to have been with me, he the following day said I was a woman looking at him with "blood coming out of her eyes, blood coming out of her whatever." This would be coarse language in a high school parking lot. As part of the national political discourse, it's unacceptable and exacerbated by Mr. Trump's pitiful invention he was referring to blood coming out of my "nose." And now he's dug out a ten-minute interview I did on the Howard Stern Show in 2010 and is trying to use this to prove I'm a wild and wicked woman who owes him, The Righteous Donald, an apology. I'll lift my dress during a Fox News broadcast before I apologize to that baboon.

It's absurd, and most ironic, that Donald Trump, who as a young man admittedly was handsome, continues to pretend to be so despite being almost seventy and fat as an apprentice sumo wrestler and crowned by a fried beaver that health authorities should impound. If The Donald's face gets any chubbier I doubt it'll fit on a TV screen. Evidently the chaste Mr. Trump was offended that Howard Stern, who maniacally drives every conversation toward sex, maneuvered me into admitting that I had relations with my husband during my third trimester and, before marriage, had "no issues" in regard to the size of his penis, implying that I've been happily hosting a big one. I wonder why Mr. Trump, a self-proclaimed Lothario, is bothered by this, and think I know the answer. So I'm simply asking, "Donald, do you feel emasculated because my husband's cock is larger than yours?"

Hillary Prays for Trump

My senior campaign advisers, an optimistic crew, are popping corks and high-fiving and whooping around headquarters as if we just won the 2016 general election. That's a long road and in the meantime we do need to periodically celebrate small victories, the latest of which is the stunning good news, for Democrats, that Donald Trump, despite sexist outbursts and unfamiliarity with all issues, emerged from the first Republican presidential debate still leading that long and eminent group of candidates, polling twenty-four percent to twelve for Jeb Bush, who lost five points, and no more than eight percent for anyone else. I'm taking a few swigs of the bubbly, too, but know our crazy good fortune cannot endure. Running against Donald Trump next year would be easy as taking on Rush Limbaugh.

Alas, my opponent in the general election will be a competent politician and therefore someone capable of winning. I'm not under-estimating anyone but tell you confidentially that, at least to this point, I'm worried about only two potential presidential candidates, the Floridians, Jeb Bush and Marco Rubio. Jeb is a proven governor, the popular chief executive of a state, like my man Bill, and is famous due not to his management of Florida but because of his last name. He is also, according to his father and brother and many others, the most talented politician in the family. For the time being he's lost amid bluster on the crowded stage, and has lamented he's a problem solver not a talker.

Marco Rubio is probably cute enough to become more popular during every debate, no matter what the polls say, but I'd rather take him on because he steadfastly supports banning abortions even in cases of rape or incest. He won't even state that abortions should be available to women whose lives are at risk. Instead, he mumbles about modern medicine providing other options. Almost eighty percent of Americans disagree with Marco Rubio about that. I'll beat the doctrinaire lad if I face him, and am already attacking, but probably will have to face the more flexible and skilled Jeb Bush.

Meanwhile, I drop to my knees, in a thoroughly righteous way, and pray to the Almighty: please let Donald Trump continue to insult Hispanics and women and his fellow Republicans and brag about his money and appall (while entertaining) most of the nation; please let him continue to lead Republican polls; please let him continue to be deluded by the extreme right wing of the GOP; please let him continue to survive and damage himself and my political adversaries. I beg you, protect this man and let him continue to be The Donald amid a group of cowed Republican opponents.

Jeb Slams Hillary on Iraq

I'm a Bush and no one understands Iraq as well as the Bushes and am proud to be the brother of George W. Bush who I still feel was right to invade Iraq in 2003. The facts proved him wrong, to the degree that any Bush can ever be mistaken about what Iraqis need, but he was right to accept intelligence reports, and ignore international arms inspectors on the ground in Iraq, that Saddam Hussein – weakened by military devastation in 1991, hemmed in by no-fly zones to his north and south, and surrounded by embargo-starved Iraqis – somehow stood at the nuclear precipice, preparing to use weapons of mass destruction on a helpless world. Thank God for George W. Bush, and George H.W. Bush, Saddam's first conqueror, and, my fellow Americans, thank God that I, Jeb Bush, am here to save you from Hillary Clinton, whose weakness and incompetence are to blame for the rampaging disaster known as ISIS.

I promise you, Hillary would be as bad a president as Barack Obama. We can't survive any more of that. Though it's politically impossible for me to state it this way, what I really mean is that we need to return to the belligerence and economic recklessness of my brother's administration. Instead, I'll euphemistically say let us not dwell on the past as we concentrate on the future and becoming stronger everywhere, especially in Iraq. President Obama and Hillary Clinton, secretary of state from 2009 to 2013, were not tough enough to admit that my brother's surge of 2007 had worked, and then when surge-saved Iraq had been liberated they lacked the strength to force the Iraqis to tolerate the presence of a residual American force that could have protected them from ISIS and Iran. If I'd been president, I would have insisted that the Iraqis grant immunity for all our soldiers who committed crimes there. That, really, is the essence of Operation Iraqi Freedom.

It's probably true that scores of thousands of Iraqi civilians were killed during the liberation, though damn few by us and never intentionally, but I'm confident that by moderately strengthening our current deployment of three thousand five hundred warriors in Iraq, we can boost anti-ISIS forces and reestablish the liberty and happiness, thrown away by Hillary and Obama, that were enjoyed by our dear friends the Iraqis. There are other things we must do in Syria and elsewhere but today I only want to focus on the quintessential issue: we need another Bush in the White House and the long-suffering Iraqi people need another Bush to protect them from Islamic savages.

Alluring Emails

Following another night of much anguish and little sleep I stumble to my computer and boot up waiting to summon emails, which are usually advertisements. Every day I hope something magic, or at least personal, will drop into my inbox. Sometimes I peer into the heavens and pray. This could be the moment. Oh, Jesus, is this real? Please, let it be. If so, it's even more than I'd dreamed of. It's an electronic missive from Michelle Kwan, the lovely figure skater I so many times watched on TV as she won two Olympic medals and more national and world titles than I can recall. How did she learn about me? Perhaps she's read some of my books or visited my website. Passionately, I click her name.

"Hey!" Michelle writes. "Have you heard? You have the chance to be just a little bit famous: We're putting up a Donor Wall at campaign headquarters, and your name could be on it!"

Examining the email I sadly determine that Michelle likely didn't send this blast. Some underling did. Michelle gave permission since she's the surrogate outreach coordinator of Hillary for America. Okay. Michelle and Hillary want some dough. They'll accept dollar donations of five, twenty-five, fifty, and so on until the box says Other Amount. I know Michelle won't much notice a five buck donation. But I can't come in with thousands. I know what to do. I Google the slender lass and note she's only thirty-five and has been in the international spotlight more than half her life. My goodness, I'm less than thirty years older. Maybe she likes mature guys. Here's a link about personal matters. Damn, a couple of years ago she married some guy named Clay Pell. I check him out. Double damn. He's a year younger than Michelle and speaks Spanish, Chinese, and Arabic. He probably speaks English, too. And he's a crony of President Obama and for a year served as director for strategic planning on the National Security Staff.

All that bad news isn't why I'm so happy when George W. Bush sends me an email. I'd been expecting to hear from him since I wrote *Echoes from Saddam Hussein*, a book about W and his cronies and the second war with Iraq. I hammered him but sent an autographed copy to his presidential library, and he's finally getting back. Uh oh, this looks like another mass email. The second President Bush tells me, tells thousands, that we "need a strong leader" like his brother Jeb who "took on tough challenges as Florida's Governor" – maybe he's referring to the 2000 recounting of presidential ballots – and "will be a tremendous President." There's a "tough road ahead" and I can help by sending an amount that begins at twenty-five bucks. You need more money to donate to Republicans, I guess.

I wish I could give candidates a million apiece so people like George W. Bush and Michelle Kwan would invite me to parties and introduce me to other influential people. I doubt Marco Rubio will invite me, either, but the following day he sends me – all right, someone on his staff sends me – an email enticing me into his "Store" where I learn "Politics is a FULL CONTACT sport." Marco's already put on his shoulder pads and helmet and is offering free shipping on all orders. Get the Marco Rubio "Let Freedom Ring" phone case for thirty dollars. Rubio T-shirts and polo shirts go for thirty and forty-five, respectively. That's about twice as much as in large department stores, but your purchases aren't backing a candidate there. The "Team Marco Football T-Shirt" is a bargain at twenty-five bucks. Number 16 is on the back, and since I'm a 49ers fan I could pretend that's Joe Montana's jersey. I think Joe's a Republican but am not sure. Though I'm not as affluent as most of Marco's supporters, I suppose I could help by purchasing a five-dollar bumper sticker for "A New American Century." His "Logo Button" also seems fairly priced at seven dollars, but I think the "Logo Mug" is pretty steep at twenty dollars and the "marcorubio" cap too rich at twenty-five.

My decisions, and yours, are very difficult. These three candidates are reasonable and attractive and politically adroit, and I believe one will become the next president of the United States. Who am I going to donate to? I'll make it clear: the first candidate who calls me or sends a personal email will get a check for fifty dollars, a hundred if the contact comes from Michelle Kwan.

THREE

Himmler Tutors Trump

Donald Trump – Heinrich, nice to meet you. Thanks for coming.

Heinrich Himmler – My pleasure. I understand you've got a big problem.

DT – It's huge, Heinrich, huge. We've got eleven million illegal brown aliens in our white Christian country, and they're murdering and raping and using welfare and in general ruining this great nation.

HH – Your dilemma is precisely what ours was in Germany after the Great War, during the twenties and thirties. There were more than a half million Jews in Germany alone and almost ten million in Europe. The Fuehrer and I were appalled since we knew all of Europe would soon be ours and the Jewish problem would be ours as well.

DT – Before we go on, Heinrich, let me emphasize that I'm not talking about killing anyone. I love people. I love the Mexicans. I love the Jews, too. I also love Germans. I love all groups. I just don't want anyone here illegally.

HH – And what happens to the many Mexicans you've deported in recent decades?

DT – They usually come back. That's why I'm going to build a really wonderful wall.

HH – Of course they come back, and no wall will stop them. That's why we built Auschwitz and Treblinka and other marvels of efficiency.

DT – I'm not killing anyone, Heinrich. This isn't World War II or the nineteenth century when Native Americans were eliminated in great numbers.

HH – In that case, how can I help?

DT – You can help with investigations and logistics.

HH – I certainly can. We'll need to identify all illegal aliens. That's quite difficult. Like the Jews, they don't always look so different from the legal aliens. We'll set up massive databases – what a godsend computers are – and start tracking them by using the last known addresses of every illegal alien in the United States. As this is being done, we'll set up elite squadrons, like our SS and Gestapo, to kick down doors in the middle of the night and send these people to concentration camps before sending them by train to Mexico and elsewhere in Latin America and wherever else they came from.

DT – You're a pro, Heinrich, but we can't have any Dachau-style concentration camps.

HH – Very well. We'll use existing prison and jail facilities and build many more like them.

DT – This must all be very humane.

HH – You're calling for the largest mass deportation in history. You must understand, there'll be some broken eggs.

DT – I guess so.

Big Crowds for Bernie

I'm having a helluva good time speaking to crowds larger and more enthusiastic than those of any other presidential candidate. Don't listen to Donald Trump and his noisy helicopter giving kids rides. He's doing okay but not like the twenty-seven thousand supporters I attracted in Los Angeles or twenty-eight thousand in Portland or fifteen thousand in Seattle and great turnouts other places. Purported Democratic frontrunner Hillary Clinton, by contrast, hasn't drawn more than five thousand five hundred. People are tired of the Clintons and Bushes and other entrenched politicians. They want something new. They want someone who understands. And I'm that guy.

Who the blazes am I? You may not know. I'm Bernie Sanders, a civil rights activist from the sixties, and a proponent of gay rights, and former Mayor of Burlington, Vermont, and for eight terms the only congressman from my state, and since 2006 a senator. I know I'm a little old, about to turn seventy-four, and look like a retired social studies teacher rather than a galvanizing political presence. I'm not trying to be a media star. My message is the allure.

I was against the war in Iraq and said at the time it would create instability in the region and not be as easy as Bush, Cheney, and Rumsfeld insisted. I hope my opponents aren't going to use my restraint in the Middle East to contend I'm against Israel. In fact, I'm Jewish and have worked on a kibbutz. My father was a Polish immigrant who got out before the Nazis murdered the rest of his family.

I understand festering problems and the danger of inaction. That's why I'm stepping up to declare we need a minimum wage of fifteen dollars an hour and that no one who works full-time should be living in poverty, and stating it's wrong the top one-tenth of one percent own as much as the bottom ninety percent and the wealthiest still want to maintain the largest gap between themselves and everyone else since the twenties, not coincidentally about the time of the Black Friday stock market crash followed by a decade of Great Depression. The rich would also prefer you not know, or at least not think about, the fact that we have the highest child poverty rate of any developed nation.

We've got to change that, and we "need to join the rest of the industrialized world… (and develop) a Medicare-for-all single-payer health care plan," and we must acknowledge that climate change is reality and caused by human behavior, and we have to stop demagogic calls, like Donald Trump's for "sweeping up" millions of people, and quit pretending a border fence is anything but unrealistic and unwise." What else, you ask? I'll tell you: racial justice. People of all colors and ethnicities must have "physical, political, legal, and economic justice." In that vein I proudly tell you I'm a democratic socialist.

Those are some of the reasons thousands are turning out to cheer as well as why I have no more than a two percent chance of being elected president of the United States.

Rubio Warns China

I'm paying experts good Republican money to write my position papers and want people to read them but too many are looking for text messages and social media silliness and aren't willing to dig into two thousand words about what my advisers think, really what I think, about the growing menace of China. Fine, that's contemporary politics. Just sit back and I'll explain the potential catastrophe and what we need to do.

China and its dictator Xi Jinping are trying to take over the East and South China Seas and cut off half the world's commerce and kick the United States out of the region. They don't like having the nuclear navy of the United States right off their coasts. What a bunch of paranoid people. Though we wouldn't tolerate foreign warships cruising along our Pacific and Atlantic coasts, the Chinese need to understand that would be different. For more than a century we've righteously sent naval vessels into other people's territorial waters to intimidate and, if necessary, attack them and occupy their primitive countries as long as necessary. I'd like to dominate China but it's too big and strong and Uncle Sam prefers to invade countries like Iraq and Vietnam, and ole Vietnam proved too damn tough so we have to be careful.

The best way to proceed is to get President Obama out of office because he has only appeased the oppressive leaders of China. We need a powerful leader like President Marco Rubio who will stand up to Xi Jinping when he cyber attacks us and builds weapons systems to counter ours and makes unfriendly remarks about Japan and the Philippines and South Korea, our democratic allies in the region. I'm not advocating we cancel Xi's visit to the United States next month, but I do believe after weak Obama greets him I should take the Chinese leader into a private room and slap hell out of him. That's the American way.

Obviously, Hillary Clinton, who as secretary of state was a disaster everywhere on earth, isn't powerful enough to strong-arm Xi or intellectually capable of lecturing me about foreign policy while I prepare to trounce her in the general election. My global insights – in Libya and Syria and Ukraine as well as China – have been exceptional, and I must modestly say that in addition to English and Spanish I am virtually fluent in Mandarin and Japanese, having mastered all but the ripest sexual phrases, and am currently fast learning Korean so I can personally, and in his native tongue, deliver an ultimatum to Kim Jong-Un.

Nuclear North Korea and China have been emboldened by wimpy Obama who, while China bloated its defense budget and expanded weapons systems, has masochistically – and I should say traitorously – slashed our defense spending and made our once grand navy smaller than any time since World War I, and reduced our army to almost the impotent organization it was before World War II. We must spend far more on defense. Six hundred billion is the puny defense budget of a weak and cowardly nation. Never mind that China only spends a third as much. China's rate of defense spending is rapidly rising. We must prepare accordingly.

I'm going to deploy more aircraft carriers and submarines in the Pacific. We also need to build "long-range precision strike systems" and to "deploy advanced missile defense systems" so China knows its navy and air force will be annihilated if they threaten our routes of commerce and those of our allies. We love our allies and they adore us and will be thrilled by my plans for "enhanced coordination between Japan, South Korea, India, Australia, the Philippines, Thailand, Taiwan, Singapore, Vietnam, and Mongolia." This is the strategic heart of the Rubio Doctrine until I need to attack someone in the Middle East.

Hillary Hoodie

got to hurry
only forty eight
hours for my
hillary hoodie
featuring blue
arrow crossing
vertical H
over my heart
only sixty
five bucks
shipping free

Saddam Battles ISIS

I know most of you believed I was a charismatic saint ready to make any sacrifice for the people of Iraq. While that once was true, I must tell you that living and golfing in Florida for almost a decade have made me soft and selfish and quite happy. I love playing the finest courses with pro golfers and celebrities from music and film and politics. The other day I played with Barack Obama.

"For years you've been lecturing us about your greatness and dedication and your willingness to lead and conquer, but that's all you've done – blabber," he said. "We need to stop ISIS and are big enough to admit we aren't big enough to get it done. So, for the final time, we're appealing to you."

"What are you going to do, break my clubs?"

"Listen, your double hoodwinked the hangman, but I'm guaranteeing that by nightfall I'm personally prepared to carry out your sentence, using a machete and three firm whacks."

"I always said Americans were beasts."

"I'm willing to permanently commute your sentence and ask only that you break off with most of your girlfriends and return to duty."

"Most?"

"You can take two or three with you. We're quite humane, Saddam."

"If so, then I'd prefer to run for governor of Florida."

"Under all circumstances, that's impossible."

"You know I can win."

"Only as Sam Sarraf."

"I don't like my CIA-imposed name."

"You're too conservative."

"Not for Florida, especially if Jeb Bush and Marco Rubio endorse me."

"I doubt they'd do that."

"I'm a Republican and a winner. They'd have to get on board."

"Really, Saddam, this political theorizing is most interesting but otherwise quite irrelevant. You'll either return to Iraq and lead forces to vanquish ISIS or I'll raise my sword."

My concentration waned the rest of the round and I hit several balls out of bounds, shattering two picture windows. As he strutted the fairways, Barack made me yearn to get him into Iraq or any other territory I controlled. That night I ordered my bodyguards to pack.

After landing at a secret airfield, I was chauffeured into Baghdad and stunned my people not only because I existed but also due to my tanned and toned physique. Each of my daily rounds of golf have been preceded by thirty minutes on the treadmill and followed a half-hour of weightlifting. Never has a man nearing eighty looked so dashing. Throngs poured into the streets and parks of Baghdad and all other cities not currently strangled by ISIS. I toured much of my country and was humbled by the love and deference I received. I shook Iraqi hands. I bowed to Iraqi women. I kissed their children. I saluted and waved and doffed my black beret.

Privately, I met with a rather timid and inept group of military officers who I would've executed in another era. I couldn't clean the stable now, and these men would have to suffice.

"I pray that all of you know the basic characteristics of our enemy," I told them. "I don't mean to insult you but must ensure you're not as naïve – shall I say as ignorant – as the Americans in regard to the nature of our mortal enemy, ISIS, which is far more dangerous than Al Qaeda. ISIS, unlike Al Qaeda, doesn't seek to occasionally attack distant targets. ISIS wants to ignore all borders and wage eternal war and acquire as much territory as possible. ISIS cannot exist in the shadows like Osama bin Laden and his wealthy associates. No, ISIS must constantly assert its brutality in occupied lands. It must enslave thousands and execute women who refuse to sexually service their henchmen, it must stone and amputate and decapitate. It must be a medieval fount of terror and fanaticism. We must stop them or they'll destroy our already enfeebled country."

"How will you do this?" asked an eager general.

"The great Iraqi masses who have just received me as a heroic leader will, starting today, be drafted into our armed forces which will grow with the righteous inevitability of the guardian of our very existence.

Worry not that any of my Iraqi soldiers will run as they so lamentably did in earlier confrontations with ISIS. We will fight to the end, and let me stress this means winning a war that annihilates all apocalyptic ISIS savages. They have no natural allies since they intend to devour everyone. Gentlemen, I promise you it is we who shall do the feasting."

Within weeks my magnetism had attracted two million Iraqis into a spirited army ready to regain our lost cities and national pride. Abetted, let us concede, by Euro-American airpower, we blasted ISIS out of Mosul, our second strongest city, we assured that Tikrit, the sacred place of my birth, would never again be imperiled, we urged the good citizens of Fallujah to quit paying two-thousand-dollar blackmails to leave, that we would soon be there, and we were. We cleansed all ISIS-infested areas, and I naturally consummated the splendid process of eviction by publicly maiming and killing all enemy survivors.

Some of my minions complained, "Doesn't that make us as bad as ISIS?"

"Certainly not. We no longer have designs on an inch of foreign territory."

Hillary Alert

team
hillary
announces
my
free
shipping
code
expires
at
midnight

FOUR

Rubio Vows to Destroy Iran Deal

I'm a warrior. If you read my recent column "Rubio Warns China," you already know that. I'm prepared to fight all over the world. In particular I'm ready to crush Iran. Tragically, the current president of the United States, Barack Hussein Obama, has "resorted to a disgraceful campaign of fear to try to sell his flawed Iran nuclear deal to the American public." He denigrates thoughtful skeptics of his disastrous plan and tries to hide its weaknesses. I think he may actually want the Iranians to develop nuclear weapons. How else can you explain the diabolical deal he's foisting on the world?

I don't care that thirty-six retired generals and admirals wrote a weak letter of support for the deal. It doesn't matter the current leaders of England, France, and Germany also support this nuclear arrangement. They are twenty-first-century Neville Chamberlains and history will damn them. History's already rebuked China and Russia, other supporters of this catastrophe, and I'm going to unveil and destroy this farce. Pay attention to the hundred ninety former generals and admirals who counterpunched their naïve colleagues and strongly denounced the deal. And trust my website and newsletter where I point by point refute those who believe Iran will be anything but strengthened and emboldened.

In order to avoid confusing you with technical details that only scientists, soldiers, and I can comprehend, I clearly explain that Iran will not have to reveal its past weapons programs and will instead turn in its own samples which is "like letting known steroid-using baseball players provide their own urine samples."

You won't believe this provision. If inspectors "suspect violations at an unmonitored location," the Iranians will have twenty-four days, at least, to hide their handiwork before inspectors are permitted onsite. During that time "Iran could easily move a small plant of advanced centrifuges without a trace."

Iran will not have to behave long because the "agreement front-loads relief" and the Iranians can soon "pocket" a hundred billion dollars, probably for terroristic purposes, and then "violate the deal" and be confident that our intricately structured sanctions regime cannot be efficiently reconstructed. Furthermore, sanctions could not be reimposed "if a European country sides with Iran…What's more, the deal allows Iran to break off the agreement in response to any new sanctions."

Keep in mind that Iran will also be permitted to "keep and operate multiple nuclear facilities for a theoretical civilian nuclear energy program, which experts agree it has no need for." What experts? I can identify them. And please ignore other experts who state that Iran, as a signatory of the Non-Proliferation Treaty, has a legal right to develop civilian nuclear energy, and also has an economic need to do so, particularly since its oil reserves are likely to be exhausted this century. I don't care. I simply don't want the Iranians to have nuclear energy.

In addition to being allowed in only five years to buy "advanced Chinese and Russian arms" – many of which would no doubt be sent to Hamas and Hezbollah and other terrorists – Iran would be able to continue to develop its ballistic missile program and "three years after the arms embargo expires, restrictions on international assistance to Iran's ballistic missile program will also end."

Rather than burdening you with more details, I here close before the actual end of my campaign paper by stating "the key restrictions on Iran's centrifuge research and development will begin to be lifted after year eight of the agreement, allowing Iran to ramp up its enrichment capacity by year fifteen, when the remaining restrictions on enrichment disappear. This ensures that Iran will have an industrial-size enrichment capability after the deal concludes, putting Iran on the threshold of a nuclear weapons capability."

My final point indicates this deal will prevent Iran from having nuclear weapons for a long time, yet I guess without a deal Iran would very soon have nuclear weapons. Maybe I shouldn't have written that, and will now have to spend even more time shouting for a bigger defense budget and tougher policies regarding China. Then, on my first day as president, I'll break the law and repudiate the deal with Iran. Don't forget. I'm a warrior.

Hillary Plans Defeat of ISIS

They're going to crush ISIS, that's all Republican candidates can say. They're going to drop bombs and destroy the threat. That's primitive and won't work. Bombing alone never works. Look at Vietnam. The United States dropped more bombs there than were dropped in all European theaters during World War II. We must be shrewder and more sophisticated, and I, as former secretary of state, understand the necessary steps. We're not going to throw troops into a regional conflagration. We're going to promote stability by helping "our partners to defeat terrorism and the ideologies that drive it."

All we need to do, after years of murderous effort, is suddenly and miraculously turn the Iraqi military into a juggernaut and transform its political institutions into sublime works of democracy. We'll also do the same in Syria. ISIS won't be able to survive or escape to Libya or Yemen because I'm going to stabilize those nations, too.

Every failure has been the responsibility of men. That's all the Republicans are offering, save little Carly Fiorina, more belligerent men. Joe Biden may come off as folksy but he's still a Democratic macho man and lacks the sensitivity necessary to weave these countries back together, actually, to weave them into something they've never been. I can do that and in so doing keep the United States out of trouble.

Marco Victory Sticker

team marco
declares another
debating victory
and for two days
offers marco
bumper sticker
with every
purchase from
marco store

Putin Assesses Carly Fiorina

Initially, I yawned when I felt hot air from the mouth of Carly Fiorina, a political nonentity running in the Republican presidential primary in faraway America. A conscientious aide had placed on my Kremlin desk a transcript of the most recent debate and twenty pages of biographical notes about the unprepossessing career of this lady who may be more dangerous than Donald Trump. At least Trump has a sense of humor and, I believe, isn't really angry. Fiorina seems inherently livid and probably hasn't laughed since years ago receiving her final inflated bonus.

My aide, who leads our team analyzing American politicians, had underlined numerous Fiorina firebombs such as, "Having met Vladimir Putin, I wouldn't talk to him at all. We've talked way too much." She's not only a loudmouth but a fool, needlessly alienating the president of the largest country on earth and commander of a vast nuclear arsenal. I know Republicans have to pound their chests in order to contend, and she's trying to out-pound her many male opponents. She also plans to "begin rebuilding the Sixth Fleet." Evidently, she doesn't know the Sixth Fleet is already a well-built and modern entity better than any fleet we or the Chinese have.

Carly Fiorina reminds me of old Cold Warriors who loved to masochistically call the massive military of the United States weak. She wants the world to believe she's a female MacArthur. She's going to "begin rebuilding the missile defense program in Poland." Really? And she plans to "conduct regular, aggressive military exercises in the Baltic states." That, incidentally, would be like Russia conducting aggressive military exercises in Mexico. Quit blustering, and think. Instead, Fiorina would rather send "a few thousand more troops into Germany. Putin would get the message." What message is that? Does the inept entrepreneur Carly Fiorina believe Russia plans to attack Germany? History escapes her if she thinks that's been the pattern. Unsurprisingly, Fiorina wants to arm Ukraine, which is not without arms now and could get into trouble if it had enough arms to behave rashly. I doubt you'll be surprised this rube is also against the nuclear arms deal with Iran. Please remember, it's not just a deal between the U.S. and Iran. China, Russia, England, France, Germany, and the European Union are also signatories. Does Fiorina think we're all irrelevant and only a Silicon Valley schemer knows the way?

This column is only a warm-up for my judo workout a few minutes hence. I doubt I will return to the subject of Carly Fiorina because she'll be out of the race by early 2016, at the latest. I'm baffled why someone who couldn't run Hewlett Packard thinks she can command the United States and dictate Russian foreign policy. Let us review. In the nineties Fiorina became the most powerful woman in business, declared *Fortune* magazine, and in part did so because she and her courtiers at Lucent supposedly created jobs and increased revenues. But subsequent accounting scrutiny revealed Lucent had been lending money to its own customers and the loans appeared on the books as income while the debt was labeled a solid asset. Granted, I have many cronies who've done that and more but few have the temerity to cite their shenanigans as grounds for taking my job, and those who do often end up in prison. But this story is not about me.

Following her "triumphs" at Lucent, Carly Fiorina became the first women to head a Fortune 20 company, in 1999 being named CEO of Hewlett-Packard. Her signing offer included sixty-five million dollars in stock, to replace what she left behind, presumably to clever accountants at Lucent, and other bonuses and perquisites. Before I highlight her record at HP, permit me, in fairness, to note the ensuing several years were a particularly difficult period for technology companies. Many CEOs, however, dealt with problems more adroitly than Fiorina. In 2001 she baffled many by leading a bloody internecine battle to acquire Compaq, a personal computer specialist with low profit margins. Hewlett-Packard, for this marriage, surrendered twenty-five billion dollars of its more profitable stock, and on the first day of this bad news lost thirty percent of its market value. Under Fiorina, HP's debt soared from four and a quarter billion dollars to six and three quarters, and the stock price eventually fell fifty percent, exceeding the declines of other major tech stocks.

The same undiplomatic and overpaid Carly Fiorina who wouldn't talk to the president of Russia, used her power at Hewlett-Packard to slash salaries, upbraid employees, order more pay cuts, lay off thousands of workers, get booed at company meetings and attacked on the company electronic bulletin board, and lay off more workers, thirty thousand in all. She also let Steve Jobs of Apple bamboozle her into putting HP labels on the backs of Apple iPods so they could be sold in stores open to HP products but then closed to Apple's. Fiorina, the one who wants to build more weapons and ships and challenge countries all over the world, thought she'd made a great deal. Steve Jobs knew otherwise, soon removing HP labels from his iPods and selling them in the same stores now dominated by Apple. Meanwhile, HP and Fiorina were for two years contractually barred from developing their own similar product.

Board members of Hewlett-Packard, quite belatedly, decided to relieve Carly Fiorina of command. This good news added three billion to market value in a single day. Rather than being mounted backward on a jackass and sent out of town, Fiorina received a severance package of twenty-one millions dollars and other gifts, rather generous for an executive who many in the industry still consider "one of the worst tech CEOs of all time."

I commend the bright people of California for their 2010 decision to reelect Senator Barbara Boxer with fifty-two percent of the vote to forty-two for Carly Fiorina, who is correct. She won't be talking to me.

Hurricane

hurricane hillary
still in hurry
loves forty
eight hour
limits this
time fifteen
percent off
everything
in store
use code
SALE15

FIVE

Trump Touts Take Our Jobs

My dense and misshapen enemies in the presidential campaign often accuse me of lacking policy specifics. That's never been true and is today patently false as to you I unveil the most dynamic dual program in history: I'm going to simultaneously eliminate illegal immigration while creating for Americans millions of jobs easy as pie to get right away.

While surfing the internet last night, looking at photos of my pre-orange-hair self as well as admiring hot babes who love me, I decided to see what the United Farm Workers have been doing. I admit, I suspected they'd been hiring terrorists,

thieves, and rapists from south of the Rio Grande. What a delight it was to read their seminal offer *Take Our Jobs* on the UFW website. It's almost as if I'd written it myself.

The UFW acknowledges "many Americans believe" there's a connection between "high unemployment and undocumented people in the workplace" and that "at least fifty percent of the crop workers have not been authorized to work legally in the United States." We are a nation of big eaters – check out my waistline and jowls – and consequently must have vast armies of farm workers. The UFW can be, and in fact aspires to be, the ally of hardworking American citizens, and made this astonishing offer: "Farm workers are ready to welcome citizens and legal residents who wish to replace them in the field. We will use our knowledge and staff to help connect the unemployed with farm employers. Just fill out the form to the right and continue on to the request for job application."

That's it. I'm going to use my magnetism to pull millions of Americans onto this page of the UFW website and thereby obtain work for them, albeit at minimum wages that must not increase if we're to remain competitive abroad, and at the same time fill jobs that are luring Mexicans, primarily, to come here and undermine our law-abiding nation.

All you job-seeking Americans have to do is enter your first and last names and email addresses and zip codes and the UFW will send you applications and you'll soon have jobs that aliens should not.

This is all so wonderful I decide to call the UFW: "Good morning, this is Donald Trump."

The lady is silent.

"I feel some tension on the line, and that's not necessary. I love Mexicans and, believe it or not, most of them love me. Besides, I'm calling to praise your extraordinary Take Our Jobs program. Can you tell him how well it's working?"

"We've had more than five millions hits on that page," she says. "And twelve thousand people filled out online applications. Unfortunately, only eleven showed up for work. And no one lasted even a week in the fields."

"Let me help you draw even bigger numbers to your webpage. Then we'll succeed."

"The numbers are overwhelming, Mr. Trump. We've made our point. The webpage is still there for everyone to see, but the application process is now disconnected. However, if you're looking for work, come right in."

Dollar Deadline

hillary's clock
ticks
bernie's books
close
carly's under
gun
marco says
chip in
jeb's dad
asks
mom does
too
now w
gives word
better
hide
wallet

Kevin McCarthy's Hillary Gaffe

Listen, I want you to know a few things. I'm an outgoing and witty guy and can charm more people than any Republican in the House of Representatives and that's why I'm favored to become the next speaker of the house. Everywhere I go I quickly rise. I did as a young staff member of Rep. Bill Thomas, becoming district leader in Bakersfield and Kern County. When I won a seat in the California State Assembly I right away became Republican floor leader. Then Thomas retired in 2006 and people in Bakersfield said the race to replace him was over before it started. I literally couldn't lose and, as expected, got about seventy percent of the vote. I've since either run unopposed or won about seventy-five percent and in succession have become chief deputy whip, majority whip, and now majority leader. No one will ever beat me in Bakersfield.

Even before I went to Washington, and especially after, people often asked: don't you want to be governor? Don't you want to be a U.S. senator? Why don't you run for president? I usually said I liked the job I had and anyway probably couldn't win those larger elections because I'm from little Bakersfield and lack the political bases of likely opponents. Really, I didn't want those jobs. Okay?

I guess now you're wondering if I really want to be speaker of the house. I think I do. I hope so. I've got the Republican votes I need. At least I had them till yesterday when I told great American Sean Hannity, "Everybody thought Hillary Clinton was unbeatable, right? But we put together a Benghazi special committee, a select committee. What are her numbers today? Her numbers are dropping. Why? Because she's untrustable. But no one would've known any of that had happened had we not fought and made that happen."

Why's everyone carrying on? Everyone knew we Republicans were conducting a witch hunt. Sure, I shouldn't have admitted it, but maybe it's better I did. Let's get things out in the open. You can have a reasonable conservative speaker of the house or a Tea Party Republican who's so far right he'll screw things up in Congress as well as the presidential elections next year. Which do you want? I'm not sure what I want.

Clinton and Sanders Shine in First Debate

I haven't seen a whole Republican debate yet since I don't have atomic cable so decide to attend a "house party" for Bernie Sanders boosters slated to gather for the opening Democratic dialogue not in a residence but a pizza joint. I'm worried. This is Bakersfield, a hot and filthy stretch of farms and oilfields and fast food restaurants in the deep south of the Central Valley, isolated by lifeless brown mountains from fresh air and free thinking. Would anyone even show up at an event organized to promote a democratic socialist who wants to be president?

Entering the dim place I look to the rear section and spot about ten people seated and already demolishing aromatic but greasy pizza beneath two flat screens showing an empty stage for debaters. This event won't be a disaster, especially since my wife and I, battling cholesterol, resolve to order salads. She somewhere discovers the bottomless croutons dispenser, but that's our only excess as Sanders and front-running Hillary Clinton are joined on stage in steamy Las Vegas by Martin O'Malley, Jim Webb, and Lincoln Chafee.

I'm sure Chafee, a scion from Rhode Island, is a distinguished gentlemen, but on TV he looks like a geezer and in this era, which began in 1960 with John F. Kennedy v. Richard Nixon, you must appear and sound presidential. Webb, former senator from Virginia, and O'Malley, ex-governor of Maryland, are fairly impressive character actors, but this is about stars. Hillary's well-groomed and relaxed. Bernie, though seventy-four, looks tough and rangy and ready to play. They've got some of the "it" factor.

In his opening remarks Sanders pounds his campaign theme that almost all the wealth is going to the top one-tenth of one percent, and the country needs more money for education. He's right about those points but doubtless also knows poor whites, who continue to be shafted by the wealthy, would rather vote for bible-thumping friends of Wall Street than someone who seeks fundamental change. Clinton, in spiritual mode and playing the friendly matriarch, says she wants to heal the nation's divisions: racial, sexual, social, and anything else expedient.

Moderator Anderson Cooper asks Sanders how he as a socialist can possibly win. Sanders repeats that very few own almost everything and the United States needs to become more like Denmark, Sweden, and Norway, which Sanders doesn't mention are small, wealthy, and peaceful countries and quite different than the sprawling and violent nation he seeks to lead.

Our Bernie brigade expands to twenty and then twenty-three adults, and two children, and members remark it's hard to hear in this echo chamber further disturbed by public address announcements: order 173, order 174... Eventually, the event organizer shouts next time we'll meet somewhere offering better acoustics and less noise.

Clinton bemoans that Sanders, a senator from rural Vermont, five times voted against the Brady Bill, which mandated background checks for those who purchase firearms from federally licensed dealers: that, incidentally, leaves a lot of hotshot loopholes for gun lovers. Hillary's husband signed the bill into law in 1993. Sanders counters the key is to keep guns away from criminals and other disturbed people. That isn't possible in a nation with more than three hundred million firearms in private hands, but Sanders has played to his constituents, otherwise he'd be a rumpled community organizer watching at home.

Someone, it matters not who, rebukes Hillary for in 2002 voting to authorize the criminal attack on Iraq the following year. Anderson Cooper asks peaceful Sanders when he would go to war. What would it take? He answers he voted to attack Afghanistan and Osama bin Laden after 9/11. When the United States is threatened, he says, not unilateral action. He points out he predicted much of the current turmoil in Syria, where Hillary tonight advocates a no-fly zone. Sanders warns that Vladimir Putin has made a mistake in attacking parts of Syria – anywhere occupied by enemies of his buddy Bashar al-Assad – and the Russian people will soon express their wrath.

Standing on stage with Sanders, a conscientious objector to the American war in Vietnam, Jim Webb, a decorated soldier in that war and former secretary of the navy, proclaims he's the most qualified candidate to lead the nation in crisis. Sanders, fortunately not armed with a handgun, responds he's no pacifist but believes war is the last resort. No one making such a proclamation, in a nation addicted to paranoid attacks on developing countries, can ever be elected president of the United States. Sanders is also precluded from winning because of his economic policies. At least he's the only non-millionaire candidate and less influenced by the tribal codes of the Beltway. Meanwhile, I'm impressed by Hillary's calm and authoritative presence.

It's halftime, and I order another salad.

The second half kickoff leads to concerns about Clinton's use of a private email server while secretary of state. She declares she's been transparent and indicates there should be no further ado about this matter. Dutiful Cooper reminds her there's an FBI investigation but Sanders rescues us, proclaiming, I'm tired of hearing about your damn emails. Let's talk about the issues. That elicits cheers, most this evening for Clinton and Sanders, and Hillary shakes her key challenger's hand.

A young black man in Des Moines appears on a screen and asks if black lives matter. Sanders assures him they do and stresses the need for reforms – how and what kind? – and offers a statistic I keep hearing but don't believe: there are more people in jail in the United States than any other country. How can China with a billion more people than the U.S. and no democracy and little free speech and a massive police-state apparatus have fewer prisoners? It doesn't. The Asian colossus likely has four times more prisoners but isn't going to report accurate figures. I digress. In the United States far too many nonviolent offenders wither in jail. Many are incarcerated because for-profit prisons lobby noble politicians to pass petty laws entrapping young people, especially minorities, and pipeline them into prisons you, the taxpayers, overpay. No one suggests that Republicans may admire the entrepreneurial nature of prisons for profit.

Sanders segues into the horrific stat no chest-pounding advocate of unrestrained markets should forget: when George W. Bush left office in January 2009 the United States was in economic freefall and about to start losing eight hundred thousand jobs a month. We're better off today, Sanders continues, but the middle class is disappearing; we need a minimum wage of fifteen dollars, and all public universities should be free.

In my notes I write: Hillary and Bernie are dominating and have stronger voices and personalities.

Wall Street regulates Congress, Bernie states. Dodd-Frank was a good start, Hillary adds, referring to the 2010 law that ostensibly strengthens financial regulation.

I jot: Hillary's getting more and more time.

The game's not quite over but I've already got the final score. Hillary Clinton, in her current form, is an overwhelming favorite to win the Democratic nomination next year. Bernie Sanders offers more desire to stop the flow of national wealth into the bellies of financial gluttons, and would be most energetic in restraining aggressive people and institutions who love to make war, but he isn't going to win the nomination, and if he somehow did he'd be the Republicans' dream opponent, someone they'd call a commie and military slacker. Bernie would outdebate his opponent, probably Jeb Bush, but he'd lose the election.

I can't imagine three Bushes, two from the same generation, being president of the United States. The alternative is therefore the second Clinton.

Trey Gowdy for President

Thank you, my fellow Tea Party Americans, I'm delighted you're inspired by my stellar work as chairman of the House Select Committee on Benghazi and my devastating interrogation of Hillary Clinton. Even Democrats concede I roughed up the former secretary of state. She should've known I would. I used to federally prosecute criminals in South Carolina, and eagerly sent away loads of murderers, rapists, thieves, and drug dealers. But I'd never encountered anyone as horrifying as Hillary. Thank God I was born brave and, even in mortal danger, stayed focused as I battered her with questions so obtuse you can't remember them and neither can Hillary. My questions weren't meant to be answered. They were designed to drain votes from her and flow into the veins of the moribund group of Republicans currently seeking to become the next commander in chief.

Though like all politicians I've cherished the dream of someday holding the highest office in the land, I concede I'm surprised, though only a little, that tonight you've come to ask that I now start making the sacrifices necessary to become our leader next year. Your points are utterly persuasive: a man as charming as I, with so delightful a voice, would be essentially impossible to defeat in any election for any office anywhere is this great nation. I accept your call to arms. Please do proceed and place Donald Trump, Ben Carson, Jeb Bush, Marco Rubio, and other guaranteed losers under house arrest, if they fail to disappear from the Republican primary and make way for Trey Gowdy.

After my eleven-hour trouncing of Hillary Clinton in the Capitol – and I so wish the process had included waterboarding – we all know I'll defeat her next November and meanwhile humiliate all Democrats who fail to kneel before the moral and intellectual might of this humble public servant.

SIX

Ben Carson's Greatest Operation

Generally, my fellow Americans, especially the whites whose money, votes, and approval I so crave, I do not operate on nonemergency adult patients without their permission. This in fact is my first time to do so, and I justify the controversial move on grounds of national security. I must as a brilliant neurosurgeon step forth and correct the flawed brain of the man beneath these antiseptic sheets. Here, my friends in this surgical auditorium and in homes around this divinely-designed planet, I present to you Barack Hussein Obama. My proliferating supporters have overwhelmed the patient's security agents, many of whom would have anyway cooperated, for the compelling reason you all know and fear: President Obama reminds me of a psychopath and that means he may well be one and I can repair him and thus, I pray, safeguard the world until I become commander in chief.

I could give you a thousand examples of the patient's psychopathic symptoms but don't want to overwhelm you with abstruse political and scientific data. Instead, I'll simply note that President Obama "knows full well the unemployment rate is not five and a half percent, and he knows that people who are not well-informed will swallow what he says hook, line, and sinker." Though he's a disastrous leader the president is without peer in deceiving the vulnerable. Like most psychopaths "he is extremely smooth and charming and can lie to your face with complete sincerity, but he knows it's a lie."

Rather than imprison or even execute him for these liberal atrocities, I shall surgically fix the problem which, in lay terms, is this: psychopaths "have reduced connections between" the part of the brain responsible for "empathy and guilt" and the part which "mediates fear and anxiety." These critical regions I shall reconnect by needle and thread soon as I've sawed open the president's skull.

Jeb Says

when
i want
advice
about
middle
east
i ask
george
w bush

Hillary v. Carly

I hate amateurs. That comes from having been a political pro for decades and getting hot as hell when I see a stumblebum like Carly Fiorina running for president, and bashing me to boot. I ordered my intelligence operatives to track and locate this hapless woman and, at the propitious moment, knocked on the door of her hotel suite. She opened, gave me the cutting look everyone else gets, and said, "What do you want?"

"I'm tired of your trash talking."

"You're lucky I talk about you at all."

I laughed. "Listen, you had maybe one half-good debate, got a bounce in the polls, and have since gone back into the obscurity you deserve."

"I'm a dynamic CEO who can energize the country."

"Like you energized Hewlett Packard?"

"Name one accomplishment you had as secretary of state."

"I had many and at this time will offer two, designing sanctions on the Iranians that compelled them to open up and bargain about the nuclear issue, and traveling to more than a hundred countries and championing rights for women. Also, as a former U.S. senator, I should remind you that I helped secure more than twenty billion in federal assistance for New York after 9/11. You got whipped in your only political race."

"Thankfully, I've moved a continent away from that liberal, tech-nerd environment."

"That was an inspired move, for California."

"You, Hillary, in behalf of the Clinton Foundation, have taken money from governments that deny women basic rights. That helped you, the only person who matters, and damaged the aspirations of women."

"All our donations have been proper and can be examined by any citizen."

"You know Benghazi was a terrorist attack."

"I know Republicans have already had their pants dropped and skirts lifted about trying to make this a partisan political issue to damage me. You should keep you panties cleaner."

Carly, reaching way back, launched a straight-arm roundhouse slap with her right hand on my left cheek – a consummate sucker she is – and I went to one knee and rightly expected a mandatory eight count. Instead, the weasel left hooked my jaw and I sprawled face down on the carpet and pretended to be knocked out, which I almost was, and prayed she wouldn't stomp me. After two minutes of groaning I rolled onto my side and Carley leaned down and said, "That's the difference between corporate warriors and political wimps."

I maced Carly in the face and, as she screeched, vowed next time to launch first.

Republicans Tame during Debate

I shouldn't have bothered taking notes during the recent Republican presidential debate. I only needed to check my inbox this morning to learn Marco Rubio had "knocked (his opponents') ridiculous attacks out of the park...Donate $7" and that "Carly (Fiorina) knocked it out of the park – again! Chip in $13 now." Evidently the GOP has some sluggers. This wasn't Hillary Clinton's show but, ever vigilant, she emailed me the "Republicans always demean and disrespect women, offer tax cuts to their billionaire backers, and leave the middle class in the cold. Chip in $1 right now." Bernie Sanders also wasn't on stage, and didn't comment on the proceedings in his email, instead stressing, "Here's the straight truth: we will be outspent." He doesn't have a Super PAC so asks, "Add your $3 recurring contribution to become a member of Bernie's Super PACK today."

It's difficult to pick a winner when ten candidates clutter the stage and scramble for air time. One man who didn't prevail was Ben Carson, the retired neurosurgeon whose opposition to political correctness and abortions and evolution has propelled him into second place. The guy who's leading, Donald "The Wall" Trump, had before the debate jabbed Carson for being "low energy," perhaps even lower energy than Jeb Bush, and suggested the good doctor may have trouble staying awake. After watching some of Carson's speeches online, I thought The Donald was being impudent. During the debate, however, I concluded the bigmouth builder may be correct. John Kasich, who's a bit of a sleepy head as well, roused himself to attack Carson for his purported desire to eliminate Medicare. Carson explained he didn't want to eliminate the program, just create individual accounts as alternatives, but he spoke as if sedated.

Trump rebuked himself for being "too trusting" but warned that if people let him down he never forgives. Thankfully, he does love the Mexican people, who doubtless adore him, too, and will continue feeling so even after Trump bills them for his wall. On this issue he's committed and isn't budging and resented Kasich's criticism, and charged the Ohio governor didn't do much to balance that state's budget since he "got lucky with fracking" and served on the board of the financial Titanic, Lehman Brothers, which "tanked" the world's economies. Kasich stressed when in the House of Representatives he, more than anyone, had balanced the (Bill-Clinton-era) federal budgets. Kasich is a skillful politician but lacks horsepower, and a bright statement from him is worth a quarter of an inflammatory remark by dynamic Donald.

Trump and Rubio were asked about their sometimes weakened finances. The billionaire emphasized his bankruptcies were all legal and corporate, rather than personal, and pertained to Atlantic City where "almost every casino is or will be in bankruptcy." He merely used the laws of the country to prosper. Rubio said his father was a bartender and his family struggled and he too has struggled as an adult, repaying college loans. He apparently could not pay the mortgage on his second home. That's okay. Lincoln and Truman weren't big bucks guys, either.

I like long shots and kept hoping Ben Carson would liven up and score some points. Many Republicans are delighted a black candidate is doing well in their conservative party, and some Democrats are also encouraged, though a bit disappointed Carson has elsewhere stated evolution is ridiculous since an explosion would've made a mess instead of creating life on earth. In regard to skyrocketing prices of vital prescription drugs, Dr. Carson conceded some pharmaceutical firms "go overboard" but expressed stronger concern about "regulatory influence…that's the problem." Trump really is unfair; Carson doesn't sleep publicly, he's just meditating.

Jeb Bush, notably more aggressive tonight than in the first two debates and on the campaign trail, was my pick to win the Republican nomination, and I'll stick with him, a hair ahead of Rubio, because I can't see who else will prevail. Either Donald Trump implodes or becomes the can't-win candidate with scant support among Hispanics, blacks, and liberals, and major problems with women and moderates.

So where will they be on inauguration day? Mike Huckabee will be a televangelist, Chris Christie a tough talker in New Jersey, Rand Paul a libertarian flower child, Carly Fiorina a too aggressive CEO of a tiny tech company, John Kasich a preacher of fiscal prudence, Marco Rubio a dreamer about 2020, Ted Cruz the same, and Ben Carson a man speaking softly for lots of dough. The Donald will return to entertainment TV, this time for a dynamite reality show, The Candidate.

Bucks for Hillary

thanks
for being
part of
team hillary
but
quick question
you gonna
donate
yes or
no

Carson Clarifies his History

I knew this was coming and liberals would attack me because I'm beating my Republican opponents and am clearly the only one who can defeat Hillary Clinton next November. The Democrats and their media allies are desperate. It's pitiful how they're scouring my 1996 autobiography, looking for inconsistencies, talking to everyone who's ever known me, asking ridiculous questions, hoping someone once saw me wet my pants. They won't find anything to hurt me. Let's clear this up and focus on the issues, which frighten my opponents.

They prefer to impugn my integrity, claiming I lied about West Point since the academy doesn't have any record I applied there. I didn't really say I applied. I didn't have to. In 1969 I was a star ROTC leader in high school and, as a reward, got to dine with General William Westmoreland, commander of U.S. troops in Vietnam, and he and other generals told me West Point would be delighted to accept me because I'd make a fine young officer. I was thrilled. You would be too. And I told many people at the time and thereafter and wrote about it in my autobiography. What's the problem?

Now there's this controversy about my violent temper when I was in my mid-teens and living in the ghetto among dangerous blacks encircled by hostile whites. You bet I was angry. But the media heroes have found some people from that period who swear they don't remember me being an angry kid. That just means they either didn't know me well or I wasn't angry with them. In my book I admitted – even then I wanted the American people to know – that I once stabbed a "close friend" and only his belt buckle blocked my knife and saved him. Naturally I used some pseudonyms in my book. I didn't want to trouble anyone or risk lawsuits.

This whole thing is a witch hunt. Liberals know that. So do my conservative adversaries trailing in the polls. They want to capitalize on a tiny error, likely a misprint, about the stabbing. I in fact tried to stab a "close relative" rather than a "close friend." Now I guess you want to know who that close relative was. A sibling? A cousin? An uncle? Who was it? Just give us a name, insist the media. I've already explained I used pseudonyms to avoid trouble. He's free to speak publicly if he wants to. I'm also not going to give you the name of the junior high classmate who made fun of me and I grabbed a padlock to reinforce my fist used to crack a three-inch cut into his forehead. Let him hold a press conference if he so desires. My mother is suffering from Alzheimer's or she'd tell you, just like you saw in the movie based on my autobiography, that I tried to hit her with a hammer when she ordered me to wear pants I didn't like. My brother Curtis interceded. Go talk to him.

Republican Picks his Candidate

Just returned from three days hiking in my camouflage uniform through a secret part of the high Sierra and had to sprint down hill, falling a few times and skinning my ass, to get home in time for the Republican debate in Milwaukee. I always love arguments about foreign policy and military matters, and knew they'd be coming, but first had to gut it out while they jabbered about domestic issues.

Some of the candidates disagreed a little about problems at home but generally they feel like this. Taxes need to be lowered so great businessmen have piles of cash to create jobs that'll someday generate profits to trickle down corporate fingers into wallets of hardworking Americans. The minimum wage must also be kept low because wealthy saviors say paying people a living wage would cause unemployment to skyrocket. That's why good conservatives still hate Franklin Roosevelt for saying, "No business which depends on its existence by paying less than living wages for its workers has any right to exist in this country." That's hogwash, just like Obamacare. Let private sector doctors, clinics, and hospitals battle each other for business so the best will rise to the top. It won't be cheap, but nothing good ever is. On immigration, the only candidate I agree with is fearless Donald Trump who still says we need to start deporting those eleven million or more illegal aliens because we're a nation of laws. He also notes, "And maybe they come back." But they do it legally.

I had a few brews to help me through this part of the debate, and told my old lady to lighten up, put away her coffee, and have a couple so she'd enjoy candidates explaining how to defeat enemies overseas and ensure our security at home.

The first guy up, Ben Carson – and I'm not saying this because he's black – is goofy as hell but fortunately doesn't know enough about international relations to talk long and only said we have to destroy the Caliphate in Iraq, and that he'd spoken to generals and it would be "easy." I admit I've never been a real soldier but have talked to some who fought in the Middle East, and they don't think it'll be easy or even possible unless we send in troops and not even most defense-minded Republicans plan to do that.

I had hopes Jeb Bush, supposedly the sharpest of the many Bushes, would be the guy who could rescue us from the Dark Ages of Obama. Instead, we're getting a whiny Jeb who irritates people, saying things his advisors tell him rather than what's really burning his gut. In this debate he said the ISIS Caliphate is the size of Indiana and we need a no-fly zone in Syria and to support the Free Syrian Army and create safe zones for refugees, all this under American leadership. That sounds fine, Jeb, but how're we going to do it without American boots? Look at the polls, folks, if we're to invade Iraq the third time in a generation, people don't want a third Bush pulling the trigger.

Donald Trump stepped up next and called the Iran nuclear deal a "disgrace" and one of the worst deals ever signed. I'm confident The Donald knows how to keep Iran's nuclear genie in a bottle. He still hasn't explained his secret plan, but I know he will. He'll be tougher than hell once he's in command of the armed forces of the United States. He's also a charming guy. He said he met Russian President Vladimir Putin before both were interviewed on *60 Minutes*, and they were "stablemates" and "did very well that night….If he wants to knock hell out of ISIS" in Syria, Trump's all for it. He's a thinking man. Americans are tired of fighting wars, and even though he's a tiger he plans to get other people to fight for us. Like millions, he's sick of Europeans and Arabs standing by while we bleed. In Ukraine, for example, The Donald said Germany should be helping since "we can't continue to be the policeman of the world."

Then came Carly Fiorina who said she'd also met Putin "not in a green room for a show, but in a private meeting." Carly's like Ben Carson, not too knowledgeable about foreign affairs, but, unlike drowsy Ben, she probably guzzles coffee while memorizing what advisors drill into her before daily winding her up to spout: she wouldn't talk to Putin; she'd rebuild the 6th Fleet; she'd rebuild the military; she'd build the missile defense program in Poland "right under Putin's nose"; she'd conduct "very aggressive military exercises" in the Baltic States; she'd put more troops in Germany; she'd enforce a no fly zone in

Syria; she'd provide weapons to King Abdullah of Jordan, who she has "known for a very long time," (maybe they dated); she'd share intelligence with Egypt; she recited a long list of Arab countries, some more than once, and promised to support them against ISIS. Carly's looking for war, and that's only in the Middle East. I think she also plans to kick China's ass. Best thing I can say: she currently polls at about five percent.

I kind of like Rand Paul but could never vote for him since he seems like a guy who may have smoked marijuana or someday will. We can't have another stoner like Obama in the White House. But I liked Rand telling everyone, especially Carly, that it's "naïve and foolish not to talk to Russia." And no fly zones in Iraq or Syria? No way, Rand says, that means we'd have to shoot down Russian planes and, though he didn't say it, that could unleash events leading to a nuclear exchange. I assume not even Field Marshal Fiorina wants that kind of war.

Marco Rubio craves the right kind of war and he's got the potential to win. He seemed like an earnest little fellow as he said he'd never met Vladimir Putin but knows he's a gangster who's using Russia's two trillion dollar economy to build up "geopolitical strength," the only thing Putin understands. Rubio loves to say "geopolitical" – that could be tough to listen to for eight years – and stressed Putin goes around beating up weaklings in places like Ukraine, the Crimea, and Syria so Russia can replace the United States as the most important power broker in the Middle East. Rubio warned that ISIS isn't only in Syria and Iraq, it's in Libya, Afghanistan, and Pakistan, and will soon be in Turkey, Jordan, and Saudi Arabia. ISIS is coming to get us because they hate our values.

I got a little loaded and can't remember what Ted Cruz and John Kasich said but it doesn't matter because I know The Donald will be a great commander in chief.

SEVEN

Putin to Obama re Paris

Dear Barack,

I know you're unhappy about my recent intervention in Syria and the Republicans say I'm a gangster and the United States must spend more money on defense and build more weapons systems to stop Russian aggression. You and I know that's bullshit. We knew it was bullshit before Friday night in Paris, and we knew it before last week when ISIS blew one of my country's passenger planes from the sky. Our biggest security threats aren't each other. Our gravest concerns are those who want to kill us and are so doing.

We must of course keep most of this letter confidential and release only parts that I subsequently authorize. I say that because, before elaborating on our inevitable alliance against terrorism, we should acknowledge in secret what we dare not in public. The United States and France and Russia have been bombing Arabs – it seems the West is always blowing up Arabs – and, though our compatriots never understand it, the Arabs are damned tired of getting killed. You've seen some of the statements online. Here's one that's rather painful to consider: "The West used to live quietly and set fire in the Muslim lands with war, but after the emergence of the Caliphate the game has changed." Let me quote another: "As long as you keep bombing us, you will not live in peace. You will even fear traveling to the market."

I'm certainly not going to publicly dignify those quotes, and I doubt you will either. A commander in chief's job is not to be honest. Our job is to keep our nations frightened and secure, even if our policies inevitably make us less secure. Let the philosophers and peaceniks deal with that. We must respond in politically-acceptable style, and we now have the opportunity to do so in a way that will galvanize our superior people of the Northern climes.

Our task is quite clear. As our great nations did during the heroic battle against the Nazis during World War II, we must again clasp hands and vow to use all necessary resources to fight and vanquish our common enemy, the ISIS hordes now so barbarically in charge of parts of Syria and Iraq. We must bomb them but we must not lie about at least this singular point: bombing will not be enough. We must put American and Russian and French and British troops on the ground, and we must do this at once. We shall destroy our enemies, and we shall resolve to occupy the region for decades and transform the heathens into people resembling the peaceful and productive Germans and Japanese, of whom we are all so justifiably proud.

Sincerely,

Vladimir

P.S. – I don't think we can do what Spain did in 2004, after almost two hundred were killed in Madrid, and retreat from the Middle East. Spain hasn't had too many related problems since. But we can't cut and run. I'm amazed Ronald Reagan survived in 1983 after he retreated from Beirut, carrying three hundred dead marines.

Trump Crashes Democratic Debate

Two weeks ago, long before the terroristic slaughter in Paris, I'd planned to attend the Democratic debate in Des Moines. I couldn't go as The Donald, of course. Everyone, even the liberals, would've mobbed me, begging for hugs, kisses, and autographs, and no one would've watched the debate. Some of my aides urged, "Go ahead and do that, Mr. President To Be," but I said, "No, I'm a gentleman and believe in the peaceful democratic process. I'll go incognito."

My crack makeup team, which has helped me look wonderful on reality TV as well as on the campaign trail, transformed me into a black-haired, mustachioed cowboy kind of guy, clad in jeans and a coarse work shirt, and by myself I took a taxi to the debate and sat in the auditorium with other folks.

I knew even the Democrats, who are generally pretty weak, would have to respond to the attacks in Paris. Bernie Sanders said he was shocked and disgusted and this country will rid our planet of ISIS. I didn't clap because I doubt Bernie's ballsy enough to get it done. On the other hand, I've got brass balls, and the nation knows it.

Hillary Clinton then said prayers aren't enough, ISIS is ruthless, violent, barbaric, and we must coordinate our efforts against the scourge of terrorism. Nothing really to refute in that statement, but Hillary lacks my international diplomatic influence to actually coordinate such an effort. She's never run a business. As you know, I understand how to bring all the personalities together as well as get building permits and file bankruptcies.

Next up came that former governor from Maryland whose name I never can remember. He said no nation is better able to adapt to terrorism than the United States, but our primary problem had been the failure of intelligence on the ground. President Trump would demand really great intelligence.

Hillary emphasized this can't be just an American fight but that we'll support those who take the fight to ISIS. Bernie said the 2003

72

invasion of Iraq was disastrous – I think that's why Jeb Bush still approves of it – and the region was "unraveled" and unstable. He proposed leading a coalition of Muslim nations to defeat terrorists, and reminded us history proves that invasions for regime change usually bring unintended (and unpleasant) consequences.

Pushing to my feet, I shouted, "Enough. I'm not going to let you pacifists ignore the most critical security measure."

Guns drawn, several secret service agents and uniformed police officers charged me. I ripped off my Hollywood cowboy hair, revealing my inimitable movie star fox top, stopping them even before I peeled off my mustache.

"Listen," I said, "I know many don't like to admit it, but the problem in Paris was the people, especially at the concert, weren't carrying concealed weapons. If they'd had guns, I guarantee you it would've made a big difference. Imagine what these agents would've done to those terrorists."

Everyone in the audience rose and cheered, and the Democratic candidates, already standing on stage, pumped their fists.

Netanyahu Campaigns in America

Thank you very much, and thank all the Americans who have so generously amended their Constitution to permit me, a man not native to this great country but who in many ways is inherently American, to try to achieve my greatest dream and become your president. I deserve your votes, and in fact am now leading in all polls, because you understand I share your core values of freedom, godliness, and white supremacy. As you know, I'm a fair man. I've never said Barack Obama is a Muslim or a terrorist or even a terrorist sympathizer, but he assuredly is a Third World weakling who terrorists know they can dominate. When I'm your president, no one will threaten the U.S.A.

Imagine what I can do when I command the armed forces of the United States. In Israel, a nation of only six million Jews armed with infinitely fewer weapons than you possess, I have still been able to devastate our enemies in the West Bank and Gaza and southern Lebanon. I usually don't even have to strike because my troops and police and secret agents oppress them in communities designed like concentration camps – or your very effective Indian reservations. While keeping the Palestinians caged, I have continued to build illegal settlements in the West Bank, creating splendid apartments on hills overlooking the land of our forefathers two thousand years ago. This land is biblically ours as it is militarily and politically ours because we conquered it during the Six Day War in 1967. I don't care the United Nations calls for us to withdraw from the West Bank and Gaza. It's irrelevant the Geneva Convention after World War II established that occupying forces may not import their citizens for the purpose of settling permanently. Who's going to stop us? Nobody, as long as the United States stands behind Israel, shoveling cash and arms.

This process will become even more dynamic after I become your next president. And keep in mind, my presence in the White House will give you unprecedented entrée into the Middle East. With Israel providing a huge and permanent network of military bases, we can easily and more often strike our terroristic enemies. When I'm president, you won't be debating what to do about ISIS. You'll be in the same neighborhood and keeping order as you please. The same pertains to Iran, which will bury its nuclear program when U.S. missiles and warplanes are permanently massed nearby. Indeed, if we choose, we can annex key strategic areas like Gaza, the West Bank, western Jordan, southern Lebanon, and the Golan Heights. Together, we can build a new world.

And I know we will. Americans trust me and enjoy inviting me to address Congress, even before a presidential election. You like the way I talk and the strength I project and know I'm an experienced warrior as well as an intrepid commander in chief. America is outraged by terrorism and tired of weakness. I share your feelings for I am you, and I'm going to continue touring this great land, shaking hands, embracing comrades, kissing babies, winning votes everywhere. This is a union long overdue.

Dining with Bill Clinton

I'm skeptical about the Clintons especially since a few months ago they used elegant figure skater Michelle Kwan to entice me to believe, albeit briefly, that she'd sent me a personal email. They haven't hoodwinked me since. When daughter Chelsea emailed saying her dad's "super funny" and a great vegetable-eating dinner companion, I knew the message was for thousands of readers and a ploy to bring in more campaign money. I remained unmoved when Hillary sent an email promising "Bill wants to meet you," and he's always a clever rascal and fine dinner companion. Then Bill himself sent an email saying he wanted to talk about what a fine president Hillary would make and added "we can talk other things," like what I'm reading since he always loves a good book.

How much did they want up front? Surprisingly, I didn't have to pay to enter so typed in my email address and zip code, clicked, and received a box of donation options for automatic entry for the next drawing along with assurance that giving money wouldn't improve my chances of dining with Bubba. I'll bet if I gave a million bucks I'd break some bread. Really, that was it for me. I'd never won anything. In my elementary school's spring fair one Saturday I entered ten cakewalks, spending more than the cake was worth, and walked around a numbered circle as music played, thinking I've got to win eventually. I didn't, not at age ten or as a young adult in the state lottery and or in middle age in Las Vegas where, frankly, I blew everything before undergoing treatment for gambling and alcohol addiction.

A couple of weeks after entering the campaign sweepstakes I got an email congratulating me for being the lucky one selected to dine with William Jefferson Clinton in a New York hotel. I'm not awed by celebrities but confess I dashed around my living room. The secret service contacted me, by phone and in person, for some general background information it no doubt already had, and I hoped my Las Vegas days wouldn't blow the deal. I guess the former president, if he was even told, didn't mind. A staff member emailed me a first class ticket for a flight from LAX to New York City, and the excitement began early on Friday when a chauffeur picked me up in a limousine at the airport and delivered me to a Manhattan hotel far nicer than I could have afforded. I immediately took a nap and later did some calisthenics before showering and dressing.

The same chauffeur arrived at seven and drove to an even more elegant hotel where I was greeted not by a bellhop but two serious men I assume were secret service agents. One said to follow them. Through the lobby we marched to a private room – impressive how many private rooms hotels have – and they gave me a pat down that happily did not include a skin search. Then, one on each side, they walked me to an elevator that rose to the penthouse. Two more guys in tight suits straddled the double doors.

"President Clinton will see you for two hours," said an entrance agent. "At nine-thirty, one of the interior agents will tell the president the time, and you're to stand, shake his hand, and depart. Your chauffeur will be waiting to take you back to your hotel."

"Fine," I said.

An agent opened each door, and my original guardians entered first and motioned to follow. I'd hoped to see an affable Bill Clinton but instead met two more agents, who glanced at my casual cotton pants and sports shirt. The entrance agents remained outside while the other four stood, not quite at attention, and asked me where I was from, what kind of work I did, was I married, and other pleasantries until Bill Clinton walked in and energized a room like no one I've seen. Grinning and extending his hand, he said, "Hello, there, Tom, great to have you here."

"Pleased to meet you."

He motioned to the sofa and we sat at opposite ends. "So you're a history teacher. You probably know all about my presidency and plenty of other presidents."

"We always study President Hoover to the present leaders."

"Then I hope your students understand my presidency was a lot more successful than President Hoover's and my successor's."

"Sir, if you hadn't been a better president than George W. Bush, I wouldn't be here."

Clinton grinned and said, "Hillary would love to meet a teacher like you."

"Is she going to be here?"

"She wanted to but can't. She's out in Iowa, campaigning."

"Glad she's working since there are so many undecided voters."

"You aren't undecided, are you?" asked Clinton.

"Your wife's an excellent candidate and I think will probably win. But I'm backing Bernie Sanders."

"Tom, he doesn't have a fraction of Hillary's experience."

"He's less beholden to Wall Street and other massive financial interests and far more likely to try substantive things to help the middle class and the poor."

"Bernie doesn't understand we can't help the poor unless we have a wealthy nation."

"He understands the top one tenth of one percent own ninety percent of everything."

"Sometimes that's about all Bernie says."

"That's what everyone should focus on."

"Hillary cares just as much as Bernie and, unlike him, she understands business."

"Bernie's the cutting edge candidate we need. That's his appeal, and his problem."

"That's the problem, all right. Bernie Sanders can't win. Do you want a President Trump? He's a charming rascal, but as commander in chief – scary. Here, let's have a seat at the dining table."

It was a round table, dressed in white cloth, designed to seat six.

A tall young woman clad in a pants suit and apron entered the suite and said, "Here are your menus."

Clinton winked at her and said, "Thanks."

She smiled at him but only glanced at me.

"We'll call in our orders." As she was leaving he said, "I guess you know I became a vegetarian after my heart bypass surgery."

"I heard. A few years ago I tried to become a vegetarian but after about a year I decided skinless chicken breasts would be all right once a week. So I'm almost a vegetarian but still have a sweet tooth that's hard to control."

"I used to be a fast food junkie. I think my body's pretty well adjusted now, though. I'm going to have their vegetable jubilee, asparagus, green beans, broccoli, cauliflower, and lots of other good stuff."

"Since I'm a vegetable man, I'll try that, too."

Clinton nodded at one of the agents who stepped into another room.

"Military force won't make ISIS end terror," I said.

"We've got to be strong. Read Hillary's website. She's committed to 'make sure the United States maintains the best-trained, best-equipped, and strongest military the world has ever known.'"

"We already have that but what we don't have, and what we need, is someone – Bernie Sanders is the only possibility, if even he's up to it – who's willing to acknowledge the obvious: occupying countries in the Middle East, and inevitably killing civilians as well as combatants, guarantees our adversaries will strike us, as we've recently seen in Paris. Furthermore, bombing them is also certain to bring a violent response."

"You're wrong, and I'll simply paraphrase Hillary on this matter. We need 'an intensification and acceleration' of President Obama's strategy in Syria and Iraq. We've got to cut off the enemy's supplies and access to the internet, and 'we should be honest about the fact that to be successful, air strikes will have to be combined with ground forces.' We, or countries in the region, are going to have to crush them."

"That's a unilateral declaration of war by Hillary Clinton, and quite strange since we've been crushing them for years and the only results are growing body counts and the destruction of their societies. These calamities ensure they'll continue to strike us in Paris, in New York, in the skies, anywhere they can. I don't think Hillary understands that. Evidently, you don't either. But you both do understand getting elected."

The former president glanced at this watch and said, "It's getting pretty late. Let's take a rain check on dinner."

Thanksgiving Candidates

jeb's sorry to reach out day before thanksgiving
but he needs my help

i'm airmailing turkey

sanders says his bernie for president t-shirts aren't
going to last

in panic i buy ten and ten bernie hoodies

as ever marco says democrats are afraid of him
they're scared of his polling numbers and fear
he'll be candidate who beats hillary

he needs hundred fifty grand in next five days
problem is marco's warmongering scares me

hillary's campaign manager says we're going
to make history and if i'm with her chip in dollar
right now

alas hillary wants war much as marco

Turkey Polls

fair and balanced
fox
on turkey day
says
its polls
prove
six gop candidates
would beat
hillary
mcclatchy
says opposite
who's deluded
bet on
fair and balanced
fox

Trump Tightens Security

People love me because I'm stronger than everyone on security and always willing to tell the truth. That's why I'm still saying Barack Obama is an alien and his birth certificate a forgery. He's a Muslim who for decades has sympathized with terrorists and I publicly batter him so other liberals can't make me rule out establishing a national database to track every Muslim in the United States. Don't listen to the disgusting First Amendment argument. The Founding Fathers thought we were a white Christian nation that owned lots of really profitable slaves, who also learned to worship our white God, and would never have granted religious freedom to Islamic fanatics who've been murdering us and want to kill many more. Trust me, I saw films of Muslims in New Jersey cheering after 9/11. Even the fat governor of that state, Chris Christie, admitted he might have forgotten seeing those Muslims celebrate. Damn right I'm going to watch those who frequent mosques.

Since I'm the overwhelming leader in the Republican presidential primary, the guys trailing me – forget Carly Fiorina, who doesn't have it – are trying to gang up, even if it endangers national security. Young punk Marco Rubio, who's always bragging polls show he'd beat Hillary Clinton and I wouldn't, said "most mosques have nothing to do with radical Islam." He's not mature or tough enough to take on our enemies, especially here at home, so he's denying they exist. A couple of other losers, John Kasich and Rand Paul, oppose tracking Muslims in this country. They know my position is right but they also admit, quietly to themselves, that they're not dynamic enough to compete with me on the same platform, so they're retreating to the far left.

Everyone knows I'm the most exciting candidate. Hillary Clinton's a flabby old woman and lacks the stamina to lead. And to those who say I'm also chubby, let me tell you, I carry my weight well and will never be matronly. I'm a man women love, and they need to accept men are in charge and obey us. Hispanics also need to fall in line or I'll deport them and bar their return with a super wall I again promise the Mexicans will pay for as punishment for sending us so many criminals and poor people. There's nowhere I can send the blacks – and I do love them almost as much as they love me – but if they are disgusting and interrupt my rallies, where thousands of people come to cheer, then they may get roughed up when my scholarly security guards throw them out. Weaklings like Bernie Sanders allow themselves to be abused during their rallies. That will never happen to Donald Trump. If necessary, I'm personally ready to fight.

Condom Cruz

ted cruz
happy doesn't
have seventeen
kids thanks
to condoms
he brandishes
before slipping
one on

EIGHT

Cruz Christmas

used to
support
hillary and
obama but
now wear
hip sweater
featuring xmas
capped cruz
smirking
under santa's
gnarly beard

Gun Lover's Solution

Listen, we need more guns. Three hundred million in private hands obviously aren't nearly enough. We need more assault rifles, and I don't mean for deer hunting, and we need millions more semiautomatic pistols. We need every adult in the country to be trained to shoot straight and pack a rod everywhere outside the home, and better keep that pistol strapped somewhere on your body even at home.

Pick up your list of mass shootings in America. You've got one, I hope, right next to your ammo. Let's look at a few; we don't have time for all of them. At Virginia Tech no way in hell a dork would've slaughtered thirty-two people if even one student in those classrooms was packing. Imagine if they'd all been prepared. Now, take Sandy Hook Elementary School. I admit, we can't let children take guns to school, though they damn sure should be target practicing after school and on weekends. If the teachers at Sandy Hook were armed, and if the administrators and custodians and secretaries and cafeteria workers were also armed, that deranged punk would've been raw meat before, or at least shortly after, he fired his first shot. Okay, think about the Fort Hood massacre. That Islamic shrink, a major in the U.S. Army, killed thirteen military people, but most were unarmed. It took a straight-shooting woman with a pistol to paralyze the bastard. Look at the church in Charleston. No way nine parishioners would've died at the hands of a racist wimp if they'd had guns nuzzling their bibles. And the other day at the environmental health facility in San Bernardino, dozens of folks were naively relaxing at a party. If even a few had brought guns to the potluck, I guarantee fourteen wouldn't have died.

There are two lessons in all this. Not only should everyone be armed at all times, we must as well have more police and paramilitary guards on duty in all places. That means schools, churches, shopping centers, government offices, large private offices, restaurants, sports events (including youth and high school), and anywhere else people gather and make themselves soft targets. These security measures will save most lives.

And another thing, don't give me any guff about our fellow rich countries – England, Japan, Germany, Denmark, and others – having very strict gun laws and low homicide rates. A few weeks ago I bet you would've added France to that list. Not now. All those weak countries, which depend on our muscle to protect them, will soon have to arm themselves internally to fight off eternal attacks by deranged losers and Islamic terrorists.

Trump Talks Strategy

Don't worry about the names of those polls, just remember they all favor me. I'll only mention one: CNN says I'll win the Iowa caucus in two months, capturing thirty-three percent of the voters to twenty for obnoxious Ted Cruz, sixteen for clueless Ben Carson, and eleven for runty Marco Rubio. Frankly, I think this race is about over. People often say I'm an amateur politician bound to collapse, yet I keep getting stronger. And I know how to increase my momentum: I'm going to keep saying things I know the majority of Americans are thinking but all other politicians are afraid to admit.

After Paris I called for banning the immigration of Muslims, and tracking lots of them, until we figure this thing out. Phonies, many of them Republicans, jumped on me. And what happened? The Muslims killed fourteen people at an office party in San Bernardino. Then some newspaper ran a photo of me with a rich Saudi and said I only like Muslims who give me money. That's a lie. I love Muslims and they love me. Many are delighted I'm involved in business in Saudi Arabia, Dubai, and elsewhere in a region anxious to have some of my great mansions and golf courses.

My Republican rivals, if they can be called that, want you to believe even if I luck into victory in the primary I can't win the general election. Trump has alienated too many people, especially the Mexicans, they say. In fact, only some are displeased I'm going to seal the border. The rest are happy I'm going to protect their families, jobs, and homes from criminals and welfare queens trying to sneak into our nation. I think the eleven million Mexicans illegally here understand I'm not really planning to deport all of them. I'm just exciting my reactionary base.

Blacks, despite hopeful contrary claims by liberals, are certainly going to support me more than they did Mitt Romney in 2012. They knew Romney was uptight and a square and not all that rich. And they understand I'm a cool guy who's screwed many beautiful women and created thousands of jobs. When I'm president, I'll generate millions of jobs, and I guarantee blacks will benefit.

I laugh when I hear opponents say I've alienated women voters. The truth is, woman have always liked me. It's something natural I have, beyond good lucks, charisma, and brilliance. My sensuality makes women want to know me intimately, and those who can't want to at least vicariously love me from afar when I'm in the White House. Trust me, I'm going to do very well with women at the polls.

People should remember the United States is still a relatively conservative country. We believe in capitalism, owning guns, having the mightiest military , and never cowering. Against the Democratic candidate, probably homely Hillary Clinton, I'll win about eighty percent of the moderate voters and almost all the conservatives. People who want a strong country really want me in charge. So does the military, which knows I'll make it even more powerful and order patriotic attacks all over the world. I'll start in Iraq and Syria to teach external enemies what my domestic critics already know: don't mess with Donald Trump.

Bernie's Gun Report

annual two
hundred on
fbi terrorist
watch list
legally buy
guns in u.s.
as sterile
senate yearns
for blood
here and
abroad

FDR to Trump

Dear Mr. Trump,

I should rebuke you for disturbing what has generally been a blissful seventy years of relaxation but understand your anxiety during the presidential campaign, a process I know perhaps better than anyone, and will openly respond to your assertion that banning all Muslims from entering the United States is the same as what I did in interning American citizens of Japanese ancestry during World War II. In fact, you further state, what I did was far more drastic. I concur about that latter point. You have no plans, so far as I'm aware, to incarcerate law-abiding Muslims who try to enter the United States. You simply want to turn them around and send them home.

There are some critical differences, however, in my orders and your proposals. After suffering a series of devastating defeats in the Pacific, starting but not ending on December seventh, 1941 at Pearl Harbor, we believed the rampaging forces from the Empire of Japan – which included a powerful army, navy, and air force – having consolidated its conquests in Southeast Asia and on various Pacific islands, would next try to invade the continental United States. I assure you, we were a lot more frightened than Americans are today. We confronted an enemy with the demonstrated ability to launch and sustain strategic strikes, and we also faced Nazi Germany, an even more formidable nation on the other side of the world.

The murder of fourteen people in a place of work in California is a tragedy, but it is not, I emphasize, a world war. I at first resisted demands to register and round up all people of Japanese ancestry, more than a hundred twenty thousand living on the West Coast. Two-thirds of them, after all, were natural born citizens of the United States. And we had very few indications any of them would sympathize or otherwise aid our common enemy from Japan.

Nevertheless, while feeling compelled to concentrate first on defeating Hitler, and continuing to watch the Japanese war machine grind everyone up, I got hit by thousands of demands from politicians, generals, and California farmers to do something to save the nation. This inner debate tormented me, and on February nineteenth, 1942, I weakened and signed Executive Order 9066 authorizing the removal of all Japanese Americans and Japanese nationals from exclusion zones encompassing all of California and most of Oregon, Washington, and Arizona. These peaceful people were for the most part taken to and housed in ten relocation camps in several western states. Others more worrisome had to live in detention centers.

Was I right to round up brown people while allowing German and Italian Americans to live normally? Now I would say no, I was wrong. But I departed in April 1945 and never had to reconsider or apologize. Presidents Carter and Reagan and commissions from their era decided "racism and war hysteria" caused the injustice, and more than eighty thousand surviving members of internment received twenty thousand dollars apiece, a small sum for more than three years of lost freedom.

With hindsight I'm telling you, Mr. Trump, be careful about using racial and religious hatred to further your fledgling political career. You may create more trouble than you prevent. In that regard, I'm holding a newspaper with photos of those who've perpetrated mass shootings in the United States since 2007. Most of the killers look like you and me, don't they?

Sincerely,

FDR

Trust

four
righteous
reindeer
pull
trus*ted*
cruz
jet

Bacon Cruz

wraps bacon
round rifle
barrel under
foil and
shoots till
grease on
floor then
unwraps and
eats smiling
like your
commander
in chief

Cruz Revolution

next two
days generous
cruz backers
offering double
your donation
don't wait
immediate help
needed for
next reagan
revolution

NINE

Fighting Ted Cruz

Look, I'm going to be honest with you. I'll soon have this nomination wrapped up. My opponents can't compete with me for reasons you should know: I was the best collegiate debater in the country when I studied at Princeton and my magna cum laude studies at Harvard Law School led to clerking for Chief Justice William Rehnquist and from there I excelled in private practice before advising Governor George W. Bush on matters legal and philosophical and then became solicitor general of Texas and prepared dozens of Supreme Court briefs and nine times displayed my oratory before the Supreme Court, whose justices probably surmised they were beholding a future president of the United States. Becoming a dominant U.S. senator was then for me a quite natural step.

The Republicans who just debated me in Las Vegas are pipsqueaks. I cringed at strident calls by John Kasich to punch Russia in the nose and by Carly Fiorina repeating her insipid phrase to deploy missiles in Poland "right under Putin's nose." I mention those two non-contenders to highlight my presidential bearing and intrinsic feel for diplomacy. Privately, I'll tell you there are only two people in the GOP race who have even a theoretical chance to beat me. No, Ben Carson is not one of them. Poor Ben should've stayed in the operating room, where he's an expert, and spared us his dreary recitations. When Ben says, "We're at war with ISIS and we have to destroy their caliphate," most people are inclined to yawn rather than stand and bear arms.

I gather you've noticed that Marco Rubio has begun behaving as a petulant child in my presence. He knows he can't be the brightest kid around when I'm on duty, or even be the best Cuban-American candidate. He's not really a quintessential Cuban American, anyway. Right, he speaks Spanish and I don't, but in 1956 his parents leisurely flew to the United States not as refugees but as émigrés; Fidel Castro at the time was himself a refugee in Mexico. Conversely, my father was tortured and imprisoned by the Castro regime and in me he imbued an unshakable love of liberty. I anticipate many personal attacks from an increasingly desperate Rubio as he watches me march away with his dream.

By now I believe the nation understands I'm most qualified to protect our lives and liberty. If I were president I would "carpet bomb ISIS into oblivion." Those who charge carpet bombing would kill many civilians don't understand that I'm talking about carpet bombing ISIS terrorists in occupied Syrian and Iraqi territory outside the cities. And like the old chubby fellow, Donald Trump, who's currently leading the polls, I understand we must ban Muslims from entering the United States for three years, but that applies only to "those from ISIS-occupied territory."

On the glittering Las Vegas stage I made it clear that The Donald and I have called a truce. I may occasionally criticize him in private but I prefer we treat each other politely until I determine the best way to disembowel him. Ideally, he'll do that job himself. Most of us, not just in politics but nationwide, thought by now he would've blundered himself out of the race. For the time being, I'm comfortable letting him catch insults for positions I essentially support such as barring Mexicans from illegally entering the United States and "getting very tough on families" of terrorists – unlike Trump, I wouldn't kill them, a difference I'll emphasize at an auspicious moment. Most portentously, The Donald and I understand, as I said in my behalf the other night, that the world would be a better place if Saddam Hussein, Muammar Gaddafi, and Hosni Mubarak still respectively led, and kept relatively stable, Iraq, Libya, and Egypt. Trump and I also believe that Bashar al-Assad, bloodthirsty tyrant though he is, represents a better alternative than ISIS, and it is therefore ISIS we must kill.

Like a patient predator I have not erupted when Donald Trump said he would like me to be his running mate. Imagine a political neophyte presuming to relegate me to a subordinate role. Sometimes I do daydream: I'm only forty-four, the vice presidency would be a great opportunity. Then I awaken and conclude, I'll still be forty-five in November next year while Trump will be seventy, older than Ronald Reagan when first elected. It's Cruz Time, and I'm ready to shut down the government again, if necessary, and attend a gun show days after the San Bernardino slaughter, and emphasize that an overwhelming majority of violent criminals are Democratic – ignore liberals who say most felons are unregistered and ineligible to vote – and I'm prepared to continue to try to defund the killers at Planned Parenthood, and ready to either refute or ignore those in the Senate or from my past who claim I'm an asshole and a fraud and wacko; I'm none of those things.

Here's the truth. Read what I'm about. I have spent a "lifetime fighting to defend the Constitution," and I've "preserved the words 'under God' in the Pledge of Allegiance," and fought "to prevent federal legislation to restrict Second Amendment" gun rights, and been honored by the National Rifle Association, and "fought tirelessly… to restore America's leadership in the world," and opposed President Obama's "dangerous (nuclear) deal with Iran," and I've fought to "stop Obama's illegal executive amnesty," and written legislation to "triple the size of the U.S. Border Patrol," and I've fought to "ensure those registered to vote are U.S. citizens," and I've often said "without life there is no liberty" and thus fought to prevent abortions, and I've "fought for the right of states to define marriage" and prevent homosexuals from ruining this sacred union, and I've fought to repeal the Obamacare disaster, and struggled to prevent "increasing the debt ceiling," and fought for those who seek "limited government, economic growth, and the Constitution," and I've fought for a hell of a lot more that you wouldn't remember except that once the weak candidates are wiped off stage I'll have more time to publicly overwhelm Donald Trump and sweep away his thirty-eight to fourteen percent lead in the national polls. The second spot on a Trump ticket is not my target, and I generally hit what I shoot at.

Hungry Candidates

emails
indicate
hillary's
unhappy
i've donated zero times in 2015
jeb
bernie
cruz
and
others
also
concerned

Interviewing George W. Bush

I'm always stimulated when former presidents contact me person-ally, as they quite often do, so with enthusiasm I read an email this morning from George W. Bush, chest-thumping architect of financial catastrophe and foreign aggression. He's a guy you can trust because years ago he swore he ran for president because God asked him to.

Now W wants another leader of that ilk, his younger brother Jeb, and urges me to donate to Jeb's expiring campaign. W emphasizes his brother has "proposed innovative solutions to restore economic opportunity for all Americans." That phrase bothers me since it implies there was great economic opportunity, rather than a gorge-the-rich collapse, when W resided in the White House, and that things have since deteriorated. I decided to call him and clarify matters. After exchanging amenities, the former president allowed me to record our conversation and said he'd be taping it, too.

George Thomas Clark – W, I don't understand how you can imply conditions were better when you were president and that, by impli-cation, Barack Obama is the problem. Take unemployment. In your final year it was about seven percent and is now about five.

George W. Bush – You can always play with statistics.

GTC – Fine, offer your own.

GWB – Lots of folks who should be counted as unemployed have simply quit looking and lots of others are just working part-time.

GTC – What about gross domestic product growth? It was only three-tenths of one percent during your last year. Now it's almost four percent.

GWB – That's damn hard to believe. Again, I think someone's monkeying with the numbers.

GTC – Here's one you can't deny. The Dow Jones Industrial Average is almost six thousand points higher than when you were in the saddle.

GWB – All markets fluctuate.

GTC – Did your policies, which favored Wall Street gluttons and home-loan charlatans, have anything to do with the financial collapse?

GWB – Of course not. My tax and monetary policies helped jobs producers accumulate wealth needed to start businesses and hire millions of people.

GTC – I wish that had happened. Let's take gasoline. It was about a buck more when you were president and we imported six million more barrels of oil a year than we do now. Why's that? I thought you were a great Texas wildcatter.

GWB – I drilled quite a few dry holes. So what? If the oil ain't there, you can't get it. I urged widespread drilling when I was commander in chief, and that momentum is a huge part of our growing energy independence.

GTC – Obamacare is reviled by many, yet the rate of those with no health insurance has dropped from about fifteen percent in your day to a little more than nine today.

GWB – It's an inefficient and expensive system that undermines the greatest doctors and hospitals in the world. That's why so dang many people don't like it.

GTC – Why are so many Republicans against the nuclear treaty with Iran? Without the treaty, there would be no way to verify their restriction to peaceful nuclear energy.

GWB – The only way to verify those Arabs aren't building a mushroom bomb, like Saddam was doing, is to bomb hell out of them.

GTC – The Iranians are Persians, not Arabs.

GWB – That's nitpicking.

GTC – When you were president, Iran had about nineteen thousand centrifuges. Now it has only six thousand.

GWB – You keep firing statistics that are probably either inaccurate or misleading.

GTC – Sorry to have troubled you with facts.

Cruz Alert

hillary
leads
army
of
rich
liberal
donors
plotting
to
raise
billions

Cruz Christmas Classics

I'm a Texan and love challenging people and foreign countries, and regarding all the crap Barack Obama has been spewing overseas, I'm just going to say: Mr. President, come back here and say that to my face, and I'll give the suffering American people something to really celebrate. In case some of you folks don't know, I'm a slender fellow and stand only five-eight but wearing my cowboy boots and ten-gallon hat, and packing a firearm, I'm a lot taller than that.

And to Ann Telnaes, that cowardly wench of a *Washington Post* cartoonist who drew my two little girls as monkeys leashed and dancing to my organ grinding Santa Claus, I say stay the hell away from my kids. I can take the abuse. My girls can't and shouldn't have to. What would you liberals have said if Obama's two daughters had been portrayed as little monkeys?

I'm awful sorry the Democrats didn't like my family's television ad that millions are already calling the Cruz Christmas Classics. They loved our funny but politically powerful titles: How Obama Stole Christmas, The Underemployed Reindeer, The Grinch who Lost Her Emails (notice how my biggest little girl delivered that line), and The Senator Who Saved America, and that would be me.

TEN

Palin in Trump Administration

I don't mind running for office because it's exciting but I hate actually serving. True, I never got to be vice president, and that's a shame for the country because I think there would've been enough fun to keep me interested. But after getting so much attention and love on the 2008 campaign trail around the country and coming fairly close to being an accident away from the presidency, I got really bored being governor and attending all those meetings and tending to silly little details in Alaska, my home but kind of the backwoods, and needed to be free to leave and star in reality TV and fly all over to schmooze with bigwigs and just regular folks who thought I was hot and a real smart politician, too.

Now I'm just relaxing and waiting for a powerful position in government, and Donald Trump has already said he'd love to have me in his cabinet. He's that kind of guy. We agree I'd be an incredible secretary of energy since Alaska's got all that oil and I maximized energy and profits and just know a heck of a lot about it. Also, most importantly, if I was secretary of energy I'd abolish the department – I could do that, couldn't I? – and save American taxpayers a bunch of money by getting rid of bureaucrats and bringing in a lot of really rich oilmen who know how to make us energy independent.

Like I told CNN a couple of weeks ago, The Donald and I are a fit and so are Ted Cruz and I. What a great problem for Republicans to have: Trump or Cruz. Either way, America will be great again. And I'm going to be part of our country's comeback. Did you see my CNN zingers? They're as good as my shots in 2008. Now I'm saying about Marco Rubio: "Robotic." Chris Christie: "Embraced Obama." Jeb Bush: "George." Hillary Clinton: "Nyquil." And I probably should say senile, too. Notice how old and chubby she's getting. And Barack Obama: "Warned ya."

Americans want more of my style so I'll see all of you in January 2017 when I join the cabinet of Donald Trump or Ted Cruz. Maybe

I'll eliminate energy before taking the job and get a cool position like secretary of state.

Trumped

thank heaven
the donald's
first tv ad
shouted islamic
terrorism and
displayed a
bagged corpse
summoning
him to make
america
great again

Shotgun Cruz

i'm not gonna
tolerate obama's
executive action to
expand background
checks and gun
safety measures
i'm gonna give
lucky protestor
engraved shotgun

Fabulous Fiorina

carly swears
poll proves
she's most
liked while
jeb claims
he's second
in nh same
place kasich
says he holds

Ted Crucifies Obama

Thank god for Ted Cruz, and I don't say that solely because I'm the man himself. I'm here to champion your divine right to bear arms and restore your security. You know you're imperiled. And after listening to President Obama's denial of reality during his final State of the Union address, I imagine you're ready to reach for the gun cabinet. I sure am.

Thank God we'll soon be rid of this strange man who's squandered eight years of enormous potential. He wants you to believe global warming is our greatest threat when in fact the whole thing is an unscientific farce concocted to undermine our free market system. Obama also wants you to think our military is stronger than ever. In truth, we have a weakling in chief who lets ISIS attack us any time it wants. Radical Islamic terrorists will tremble when Ted Cruz takes residence. Remember, an Iran emboldened by Obama's doomsday surrender is preparing a nuclear strike. Only liberals believe the treaty and onsite inspections will deter the barbarians.

Thank Heaven we're evicting Obama from our chicken coop and will have a leader who can restore jobs and growth. How dare he stand up there, in the Congress of the United States, and claim we have the strongest and most durable economy in the world and the auto industry just had its best year ever and anyone who claims the U.S. economy sucks is peddling fiction. Those falsehoods fly right out of the liberal playbook. Obama brags about cutting unemployment in half, but he doesn't count those who no longer look for work, he pretends they don't exist.

Believe me, we're a sick and weakened country. We're only spending more on defense than the next eight countries combined. We used to outspend the rest of the world. We need to invest more or those terrorists Obama calls "fighters in backs of pickup trucks" will threaten our existence. Though he speaks sternly about "fanatics who have to be hunted down, rooted out, and destroyed," Obama does little but whine we "can't carpet bomb civilians" and we "can't rebuild every nation in distress."

Too many nations have suffered because of Obama's weakness. Strength will return when I become commander in chief.

Hillary Bernie Battle

race tightens
and hillary
calls bernie
friend of nra
he counters
she feeds on
wall street

ELEVEN

Cruz Arousal

cruz
writes
scared
gop
attacks
to
ruin
campaign

Palin for Trump

next
time
palin
endorses
please
sit
down
so
voters
can't
see
you
grimace
and
squirm

Candidates in Need

campaign treasurer
emails he's going to
tell jeb i still haven't
donated marco's director
needs immediate help to
destroy obama legacy
today hillary only wants
a buck to stop big spending
bernie carly still freezing
ass in essential iowa

Marco's Faith

atheist
asks
marco
if
running
for
pastor
in
chief

Anxious Cruz

urgently writes
nowhere else
to turn stakes
never higher
send money
now

Trump Fires

the donald
could shoot
someone in
middle of
fifth ave and
still become
terrorist in
chief

Trump Delight

really
rich
guy
savors
his
fanny

TWELVE

Cruz to Iowans

you must decide
who
will kill terrorists
who
will defend constitution
who
will repeal obamacare
who
will secure borders
who
will defend life
examine
our records and
pray

Terrific Trump

i terrify
world leaders
and guarantee
they'll follow
my commands
when megyn
kelly quits
bullying me

Revelation

news flash
bernie
doesn't
like
billionaires

Little Iowa

Late last night and early this morning the celebratory emails have come pinging in. Marco Rubio exclaimed, "We did it. What a night. The outcome was amazing. The media and the establishment had counted (me) out." He finished third in the Republican Iowa Caucus, earning twenty-three percent of the vote and seven delegates. Ted Cruz asserted, "Last night was a victory for the grassroots, and for the millions of conservatives who are rising around the country." He received twenty-eight percent of the vote and eight delegates. The guy who finished second, Donald Trump, didn't send me an email, and it's possible his web techs have taken me off their email list since I've written, and sent them, some uncomplimentary characterizations of their star. Though The Donald has endlessly proclaimed himself the ultimate winner in life, and at the moment is less than that, he doesn't need to cry, yet. He took second place and seven delegates.

Trump probably would have won had he not skipped the final debate and convinced most late-deciding Iowa voters that Cruz or Rubio was their candidate. If the bully from New York City loses in New Hampshire, an unlikely event, he'll be up to his waist in quicksand. And if he loses among reactionary Republican voters in South Carolina, even more improbable, he'll have to be pulled out by his ears and quit the race. This may be what Donald Trump wants, to escape the firestorm he created. He looks exhausted, his eye bags darkening by the week as learns people you hit generally hit back. He'll have to pick some other states where he can take a dive.

I still haven't determined why Carly Fiorina declared, "We're surging," in reference to earning two percent of the vote.

Following the Democratic Iowa Caucus, Bernie Sanders stated, "Tonight we accomplished the impossible...The people of Iowa sent a very profound message...It is too late for establishment politics and economics in this country." Perhaps anti-establishment rebels Bernie and Marco would make an invincible duo in the general election.

Bernie probably won't get there, especially since Hillary Clinton clobbered him by three-tenths of a percent and twenty-two delegates to twenty-one, and rejoiced, "Our team had a historic win in Iowa last night" – the first time a woman has won this overhyped political event.

Here are the three most relevant questions:

1. What is Iowa? It's an agrarian Midwestern state of about three million people, less than one percent of the nation's total. Eighty-seven percent of the population is white, three and a half percent African American, two percent Asian American, and about five and a half percent Latino. The national breakdowns are respectively quite different: sixty-two percent white, thirteen percent African American, five and a half Asian American, and seventeen percent Latino.

2. What the hell is the Iowa caucus? Only the most dangerous political wonks can concisely answer that one. I'll quote Wikipedia: "The caucus is an electoral event in which residents of Iowa meet in precinct caucuses in all of Iowa's one thousand six hundred and eighty-one precincts and elect delegates to the corresponding county conventions. There are ninety-nine counties in Iowa, and thus there are ninety-nine conventions." There's more, but let's move on.

3. What does losing the Republican Iowa Caucus mean? It doesn't amount to much more than a few piles in the cow pasture. In 1980 Ronald Reagan finished second, to George H.W. Bush, yet won the primary and two presidential elections. In 1988 Bob Dole conquered Iowa but third-place-finisher Bush captured the primary and general elections. In 2008 Mike Huckabee took first, trouncing fourth-place finisher and eventual nominee John McCain by more than twenty percent. Four years ago Rick Santorum nipped Mitt Romney, who would win the nomination.

Bring on the main events, and, no, they ain't New Hampshire and South Carolina.

New Hampshire Speaks

After many months of hot-air speeches, crowded debates, unpleasant sound bites, insulting advertisements, and inane emails, we at last had a real election, two in fact, as tiny New Hampshire sent a sliver of its one point three million souls to the presidential primary polls. Though we respect the Iowa caucuses, and The Hawkeye State's abstruse political customs, we really can't count that process as a democratic election. Thus, the state where residents Live Free or Die retained the honor of voting first, and probably shall for decades to come, though that task – shaping the early course of selection – would more logically be served in populous states such as California, Texas, and New York.

In the current system there came from New Hampshire a warning from landslide-victor Bernie Sanders that "our victory tonight will prompt a desperate response…We sent a message that will echo from Wall Street to Washington, from Maine to California." I assume Bernie anticipated attacks from big-bank Hillary Clinton, an athletic sort, who said she "knows what it's like to be knocked down," and hitting the deck isn't what matters; "It's about whether you get back up." Hillary seemed quickly on her feet, stressing she daily practices "the discipline of gratitude… (She's) grateful not just for the good things – that's easy – but the hard things, too. (She's) thankful for the seven hundred thousand people…who've given to this campaign," and I'm wagering she's grateful in two and a half weeks she gets to fight Bernie in South Carolina where she leads by thirty points. The Vermont socialist, who speaks Brooklynese, will have to quickly convince Southern blacks and less-than-liberal whites his policies will help them more than Republican largesse for the wealthy.

Many Republicans prayed devilish Donald Trump's narrow loss in Iowa would clear the runway for Marco Rubio or another less toxic candidate to change the GOP's trajectory. The Donald crushed that establishment notion, winning by nineteen percent over John Kasich and a few more points against Ted Cruz, Jeb Bush, and the suddenly flustered Marco. Before the election, in a debate exchange with Chris Christie, Marco twice recited the same (at that moment irrelevant) charge that Barack Obama is trying to turn the United States into a Third World backwater. Many viewers booed and hissed, and poor Marco, the almost-anointed one, instantly became the "robotic" kid who still can't hit a major league fastball.

Trump didn't boast. He let the *Washington Post* do so, on his website, with the headline: "Donald Trump Loves Winning, and He Won Just About Every Group in New Hampshire." He also posted the *Wall Street Journal* article announcing his victory by a "decisive margin." Always anxious Ted Cruz wrote, in a "personal" email, that the "Washington Cartel is in a panic." He didn't mention that Trump had trounced him by twenty-three percent. Actually, Cruz feels this panic is due to the ardency of his backers who he dares to "make conservatism mean something again…HERE'S THE DEAL: we are just eleven days away from the tipping point – the South Carolina primary." Tense Ted currently trails The Donald by sixteen points in The Palmetto State and is unlikely to get much closer, despite the self-acclaimed significance of his victory in the Iowa Caucus.

Jeb Bush celebrated his fourth place finish, proclaiming, "Last night was an important step, and I can't thank you enough for your help in getting us there. But, the real fighting begins now. South Carolina is three times the size of New Hampshire." That probably means a bigger whipping for Jeb since he trails Trump by twenty-six percent there. In his home state of Florida, where as governor he shaped the disputed outcome of the 2000 presidential race, Jeb lags by thirty-one points. Voters must still be disenchanted he still clings to his brother's legacy of criminality and failure. Really, Jeb lost this presidential race in 1994 when he dropped a close contest in the Florida gubernatorial race. Had he won, he would have been reelected in 1998, and probably would've been the chosen one – instead of W – to run against Al Gore in 2000. Of course, Jeb wouldn't have been at the helm in Florida to tinker with election results, so it's unclear if he would've become president.

Sensing he'd fanned with the bases loaded in the debate, Marco Rubio early on election morning in New Hampshire ordered his communications director release this fatuity: "The liberal media tried to create a false narrative to try to slow down Marco's campaign in the final days" before this primary. Later, cradling about ten percent, Rubio acknowledged, "I dropped the ball Saturday night." He could've said balls – baseballs, footballs, basketball.

John Kasich, seemingly a decent and competent politician but also one who in a debate several weeks earlier urged the United States to "punch Russia in the nose," was transported by finishing a weak second, and announced he was "surging" and Jeb was "attacking" him and "distorting" his record. Jeb isn't his most immediate problem. Big John's polling about two percent in South Carolina, to Trump's thirty-six, and neither Jeb nor the Russians are to blame for that.

Cruz Can

friend
let me
be blunt
i can beat
hillary but
donald can't

THIRTEEN

Trump Documentary Thrills Voters

Thank God for Donald Trump and FunnyOrDie.com, the website now showing the most important documentary film ever, *Donald Trump's The Art of the Deal: The Movie,* a penetrating study of The Donald, young in the nineteen eighties, that convinces me Ted Cruz and Marco Rubio, no matter how wonderful they may be, are not ready to be president. Only Trump is qualified, and I'm ashamed I hadn't perceived that before viewing this previously-lost work purchased at a Phoenix yard sale by a bargain hunter named Jenny who was subsequently robbed of the treasure by Ron Howard, a scraggly-bearded guy you probably haven't heard of. He's better known as little Opie from *The Andy Griffith Show.*

If The Donald's documentary wasn't preempted in 1988 by liberal fools who instead broadcast a meaningless Monday Night Football game, he likely would've been propelled to the presidency that very year as Americans followed his beat like they do today. On film behold the compassionate tycoon as he allows a boy, who stole his bestselling book *The Art of the Deal,* into his lavish office to witness phone conversations with Merv Griffin and Lee Iacocca and his father, who he orders to curse reprehensible Mayor Ed Koch of New York. Despite high pressure deal making, Trump has time to tell the lad his father wasn't heroic for dying in Vietnam. It's "more heroic" not to die. The budding billionaire had draft deferments to protect his and the nation's interests. He knows how to operate. Even in the eighties he considers the homeless a menace, and is proud to avoid renting to blacks since "in America everyone should be able to be priced out of his own neighborhood."

While discussing big deals in a bar, the other man tells Trump, "No sleeping with other men's wives…You're so good looking…great hair…cool teeth…a big hairy dick." The Donald good naturedly agrees, and in a similarly charming way tells his Jewish lawyer to show the kid how he, the lawyer, bit off the cock of an enemy. That reminds

Trump: he's got to acquire the Taj Mahal casino in Atlantic City, and prissy Merv Griffin doesn't want to sell. The NFL, led by its "fat sweaty turd" commissioner Pete Rozelle, is also being unjust, trying to maintain a monopoly. The Donald yanks them into court, sues for antitrust violation, and wins the case. Shockingly, his reward is but a single dollar.

Blonde and beautiful Ivana Trump enters her husband's sanctum, and he proudly says she runs Trump Castle in Atlantic City. However, when she tries to talk The Donald quiets her, and she smiles in ongoing gratitude that such a man has married her, an immigrant who understands why Trump considers Merv Griffin more important. He's telling Merv he doesn't want the Taj Mahal while he studies blueprints for gorgeous changes. Meanwhile, The Donald dismisses the first kid, Jose, as well as his replacement, an Asian kid, and the next one, too, a black kid. They've got another now. Kids don't matter in this film. They're extras.

The Donald announces he's always wanted to do two things on Fifth Avenue: shoot someone and build a fabulous building. He probably hasn't done the former but he creates Trump Tower after telling Tiffany's, "You've got this place loaded with Mexicans," and shows his rivals how he'll cover their building with graffiti if they cause trouble while he's building his classy tower, which has to be stripped of old friezes and other unsightly artworks that are destroyed rather than cause a construction delay. During this period, after sitting on his commode and reading *The Art of the Deal,* Merv Griffin reveals he's ready to sell the Taj Mahal.

Summarizing the documentary, which he writes, produces, directs, and stars in, The Donald says that "life is a series of deals, and the key is to win them." He reminds us he's ready to "fuck the other party" and foreigners, and the only thing that matters is Donald Trump.

Flint Water

flint
officials
swear
brown
water's
just
fine

Trump Conquers South Carolina

People of South Carolina standing before me, and to everyone all over the world watching on television, take a look at my family, will you? My wife Melania's gorgeous and could be my daughter and my daughter Ivanka's a supermodel even though she may have another kid as I speak. And look at those two blonde babes married to my sons. They're terrific. And way out there to your right is my youngest daughter, Tiffany, another blonde bombshell. I sired her with my second wife, Marla Maples, who's also quite hot, but we don't have room on stage for her or my first wife, Ivana. They got a little too old for me but understand that and still love me. I think love is my secret. I love all groups. I love Mexicans and Muslims and Chinese and Democrats, which is really what I used to be, and of course I love Republicans, especially those in South Carolina who've basically just handed me the presidency, voting me to a ten-point victory over those wonderful young Cuban Senators Marco Rubio and Ted Cruz. I don't know which of them is going to get second place here. It doesn't matter. They'll both soon be heading back into obscurity.

I'm not going to mention Governor Nikki Haley by name. She's hot but she's a loser. She endorsed Rubio. The winner, Lieutenant Governor Henry McMaster, and his pretty blonde wife, supported me and get to stand on stage as I thank South Carolina for moving me closer to the power I need to make America great again. We never win anymore. China kicks our asses and picks our pockets in trade and so does Japan and of course Mexico does too You remember that historical day last June in fabulous Trump Tower when I promised you that Mexico is going to pay for the wall I build between our two countries. And let me ask you right now, who's going to pay for it? Mexico, you shout. That's right. We have a trade deficit with them of almost sixty billion dollars, and the wall will only cost about twelve billion, so believe me they're getting a great deal and I won't listen to their complaints.

I'll be busy overturning Obamacare and replacing it with something much better and far less expensive. You don't need the details now. Trust me. It'll happen. American's going to be better than ever. I'm going to transform education in this country. How? Just wait and see. And I'm going to rebuild our military so that we're no longer a defenseless weakling who everyone attacks. I feel all these great changes happening as my presidency approaches. Hillary Clinton knows it too. She barely beat socialist Bernie Sanders in Nevada today. She's a weakling I'll bounce around like I do these Republican stumblebums.

Trump Prepares for Coronation

Folks, it's just about over and, having dispensed with the gnats in my ears, I'll soon be able to concentrate on whipping Hillary Clinton's fat ass and making America special again. If you doubted me before the Republican debate in Texas, I'll bet you don't now. Let me tell you about the polling right afterward, but first let me tell you about my performance.

Marco "The Runt" Rubio, still staggering after his psychotic repetitions during the New Hampshire debate, followed orders of those who lead him by a leash and attacked me because I'm the overwhelming leader in almost every state in the union. He said I was weak on immigration. Please. I countered that after former Mexican President Vicente Fox used a "filthy, disgusting" word to describe my wall on the border, the wall "just got ten feet taller." Notice that what once seemed to some an outrageous claim – I'll make Mexicans pay to wall themselves in – is being cheered by increasing numbers of Americans tired of losing to Mexico and everyone else.

Rubio also claimed I didn't support Israel. I responded that not only do I love Israel, I've won more awards there than I can count. The Israelis also love me, and so do New York Jews. For that matter, Hispanics love me and that's why I won about forty-five percent of their vote in Nevada. I'll continue to do well with them because they know I'm going to protect their homes and create jobs. I actually hire people. I've hired tens of thousands in my legendary business career. Marco Rubio's never hired anyone. He bought a house for a hundred eighty grand and sold it for twice that to a lobbyist who was probably in the hall cheering the snotty little senator. That's his idea of business.

Desperate, and heartened by a few cheers probably led by his sugar-daddy lobbyist, Rubio accused me of inheriting two hundred million dollars. That's not true. I only borrowed one million little dollars and then made my fortune by building fabulous buildings and wonderful companies. Do you think Marco Rubio could've done that?

Get serious. Few paid attention when he accused me of repeating myself like terrified Rubio did in New Hampshire. I wasn't repeating myself. I always remain cool before counterpunching attackers, and pointed at Rubio and told him he's a "choke artist" and "pouring sweat" like no one I'd ever seen. Guys like that can't change and are chokers for life. He's not tough or smart enough to make deals. I'm a great deal maker. That's why I'm trouncing him in the polls in Florida. He can't win anywhere, even at home. Then I pointed at poor Ted Cruz, who I may beat in his state of Texas, and told him he's a "liar." A little later I said, "You're a basket case."

Jeb Bush, another weakling from Florida, who's now home watching on TV, warned me that I "couldn't insult my way to the presidency." Wanna bet? Despite many pundits hyperventilating that Marco Rubio won this debate, my people jumped online and checked *Drudge* and *Slate* and the *Wall Street Journal* and the *Austin American-Statesman* and many others to learn who people around the country think won. Most polls showed seventy-eight to eight-five percent thought I prevailed. Drudge was way too low, giving me only sixty percent. But you get the point. Super Tuesday's in a few days, and a couple of weeks after that I should effectively have the nomination. Republicans everywhere are making it clear: they want Donald J. Trump.

Super Trump Tuesday

Before dealing with petty attacks against my character and candidacy, let's emphasize the primaries just resulted in Super Trump Tuesday as I won seven states to three for Lyin' Ted Cruz and one, finally, for featherweight Marco Rubio. I've got more delegates than both combined. Rubio's not strong enough to beg others to leave the race. Neither is Cruz but he's asking anyway, claiming all abandoned voters would rush to him to stop Donald J. Trump from ruining the Republican party while getting trounced by Hillary Clinton in the general election. Keep in mind, folks, Ted Cruz is the most unpopular member of the Senate and has precisely no endorsements coming from any of his ninety-nine colleagues. Cruz makes them miserable and they know he'd be insufferable in the White House, which he's incapable of winning anyway.

I'm the only Republican who can win now, and I'm certainly the only candidate who can stop the Clinton machine in November. In a couple of weeks I'll effectively clinch the GOP nomination. I'm leading in Florida, Rubio's home state, by almost twenty points, by about fifteen in Illinois, ten in North Carolina, and around five in Ohio, home of snoring John Kasich. Meanwhile, next week, I'll rake in many more delegates in Michigan, where I'm up by twenty. Do the math. Ted Cruz has. So have some Republican politicians and their cronies in the conservative media. They don't want me to break up their all-talk no-action old fogies club. But they've got a problem. I'm more dynamic and politically gifted than they ever imagined. Frankly, I didn't know I was so appealing, either, or I'd have become president long ago. I feel bad I didn't run in 2000 and save the country and the world from the low IQ aggression of George W. Bush. At least I booted his brother Jeb.

Now, just before the field shrinks to two candidates – Hillary Clinton and Donald J. Trump – I'll address two of the many filthy attacks recently initiated by the Republican establishment. During an interview

I was asked about the KKK and its former grand wizard David Duke, who's passionately supporting me. My damn earpiece – the one the network gave me – wasn't working properly and I should've stood up and fired those responsible. Instead, I said I'd never met David Duke. Really, I haven't. If the electronic buzz in my ear hadn't confused me, I would've denounced Duke as a bad guy. A couple of days later I roughed him up like I do all difficult people. Don't blame me for David Duke and the KKK, which is a group of nasty people. What my opponents are learning, though they try to portray me as a fascist, is that I love people. I love all groups, and they know that because thousands of them work for me and earn great wages.

Really, I pity Ted Cruz and Marco Rubio, who I used to like but lately he's been getting dirty and calling me a dangerous con artist. I guess that's what a hyperactive choker says about the guy who's trouncing him in his home. Rubio, like all politicians, except me, doesn't understand that deals have to be made. I'm going to send him a copy of *The Art of the Deal*. Then he'll understand that though I love Israel there are two parties in the neighborhood and both, including the Palestinians, need to be equal partners in any negotiation. Rubio and Cruz also need to learn not all my comments about immigration should be taken literally. I suppose you've heard I gave the editorial board of the *New York Times* what I thought was an off the record interview. And, yeah, I said maybe I'm not really going to deport all eleven million illegal aliens. That number is just a starting point for negotiations. You have to start high because you can always lower your demands but can't start low and go up. Gravity doesn't work that way.

I know you're sick of Ted Cruz and Marco Rubio and John Kasich and Hillary Clinton, who'll effectively finish off Bernie Sanders pretty soon. Don't worry. It'll just be Hillary and me and you'll be amazed what I do to her.

FOURTEEN

Abe Lincoln at the Republican Debate

Abraham Lincoln – I'm a man tired and saddened by four years of bloody civil war that ceased only yesterday but am honored to move forward a century and a half and moderate my Republican Party's debate to determine the next president of these, our unvanquished, United States. The lovely and gracious Megyn Kelly has privately briefed me about you four gentlemen, and I figure I'll have a sense about what's right.

Let me start by asking the man currently atop the polls, Mr. Donald Trump, if it bothers him his hands are so awfully small.

Trump – Abe, I have very powerful hands and, I must tell you, I'm quite a stud, to use modern terms I'm sure a man of your brilliance can figure out.

Lincoln – From where I stand, six-foot-four and blessed with the eyesight of an eagle, I must tell you, sir, that your hands appear rather stubby, like the nubs of my infamous rhetorical adversary, Stephen Douglas, who I heard, more than once, was not particularly well endowed. I trust you wouldn't prevaricate about such an essential matter before the American people.

Trump – Abe…

Lincoln – It's the next man's turn, Mr. Trump. Senator Marco Rubio, you're just a bean sprout of a fellow and I reckon aware I could whip you in wrestling.

Trump – He's a very little man. Call him little Marco, the choke artist.

Marco Rubio – I want you to know, President Lincoln, that I admire you very much and readily concede you could beat my ass wrestling or in any other form of combat except a shootout with automatic rifles, which, admittedly, you've never had a chance to practice with.

Lincoln – I've just presided over an unspeakable national tragedy and seek to avoid armed violence, Senator Rubio. Now, Senator Ted Cruz, you appear to be only a little taller than Senator Rubio. Do you suffer from a Napoleonic complex? I understand your colleagues in the Senate consider you the backside of a mule.

Ted Cruz – They're jealous of my eloquence, President Lincoln, and know I'm by far the finest debater to run for president since that tall and majestic man from Illinois, the very Abe Lincoln who today graces us. Regarding my height, I frankly feel like a giant whenever I'm in a room with the junior Cuban American in the Senate, Marco the Midget.

Lincoln – Governor John Kasich, I almost forgot about you and that's probably why you're last in the polls. May I ask if any of your body parts are unusually short or otherwise inadequate?

John Kasich – President Lincoln, I'm the grown-up on this stage tonight, utterly comfortable with all my organs and appendages, and for that reason am most prepared to debate the issues.

Lincoln – I'm tuckered out by issues, gentlemen. None of you have shouldered the calamities and responsibilities of a man trying to save the nation.

Trump – You're not looking good at all, Abe.

Lincoln – You're a pretty strange looking fellow, too, Donald. I don't recall ever seeing a man with either an orange face or orange hair, and you've got both. You're also rather matronly.

Trump – I've got billions of dollars, Abe. Have you seen my wife? I'm afraid I've seen photos of yours.

Lincoln – Are you insulting Mrs. Lincoln?

Trump – Abe, she's a barker. A man in the White House should do better.

Megyn Kelly – Donald, that's precisely the type of crude misogyny that's finally galvanizing the nation against your candidacy we all realize is founded on spreading hate and fear.

Lincoln – Most beautifully stated, Mrs. Kelly.

Kelly – I'm single, President Lincoln.

Trump – You're married, Megyn. Show some morals.

Kelly – We're separating.

Lincoln – Is your husband inadequate?

Kelly – He's all right, but I have a more important duty, preparing you to run as president in place of these clowns.

Hillary Mulls VP Choice

My following remarks are to stay in this room, that is, they're to stay inside your heads once we leave this room. If anyone leaks my strategic utterances, I'll find out and you'll regret it. Understood? Fine.

Clearly, after March fifteenth, I will be the inevitable Democratic nominee for president of the United States. If I weren't such a shrewd and disciplined politician I'd claim victory now. But I won't. For a week or so I'll let Bernie Sanders and his young and naïve socialists pretend this nation doesn't need Wall Street and war to flourish. I'm an ass kicker and our enemies better beware.

Look at the math. I'm up by forty points in Illinois, thirty in Florida, and twenty in Ohio. It's going to be just as bad for Bernie today in Mississippi and Michigan. After this slaughter, he'll have to drop out of the race so I don't have to travel and spend so much. I want to kick back and get ready for Donald Trump or Ted Cruz or whatever bozo the retrograde Republicans send into the ring. But I'm worried Bernie believes he's running more than a campaign, he's leading a movement to pull us moderate Democrats into loony-land. He better stop once I apply my electoral chokehold. If he behaves, I'll offer him the vice presidency. We'd have his hot-blooded kids and my blacks, Latinos, women, centrists, militarists, and hedge fund managers. We'd be a juggernaut, and I'd get about sixty percent of the vote, and we'd reoccupy the Senate and the House.

However, if Bernie won't play Hillary ball after the Ides of March, then I may exile him. I'm still not sure the best way to do that since he raised forty million bucks last month and has more than five million donors. I may have to let him enjoy his power rush a little while longer. I'm betting Bernie fears returning to the slow life of an obscure senator from Vermont more than he dreads serving as my high-profile caddy for four years, eight if he looks like he can roll until age eighty-three.

Commander Cruz

cruz campaign
announces
strong second
place finishes
in mississippi
and michigan
followed by
victory in idaho
and carly fiorina
endorsement
prove remarkable
national momentum
will make ted
commander cruz

Hillary-Bernie Debate Party

"Have a beer," says Ed, host of the Hillary-Bernie debate party at his house.

"No thanks, gave it up years ago," I say, and walk into a living room full of revelers watching giant-screen images of foxy Megyn Kelly and happy Ted Cruz, a smiling gentleman unlike the notorious senator who's provoked Republican colleagues to discuss devious ways of torturing him.

Among this group of presumed Democrats in Kern County, I'm reluctant to say, "I think these two have a bit more star power than Clinton and Sanders. Let's stay here a while."

Ed summons CNN which teams with Jorge Ramos and Maria Elena Salinas of Univision to host the event. Immigration is a key topic. Hillary's asked if she would become the next deporter in chief, like President Barack Obama, who has presided over two and a half million people being returned to Mexico. Hillary vows to concentrate on terrorists and violent criminals, but that's not what's being asked. Will she promise not to deport children or adults who have no criminal records? She agrees. Sanders says Obama's wrong on deportation and also seconds Hillary's promise. Donald Trump, by contrast, wants to uproot eleven million undocumented Mexican nationals and send them south.

Hillary denies she sought to construct a wall several years ago and resents being tied to barrier-obsessed Trump. She says she only wanted a fence in a few areas and more guards in others. Bernie notes the *New York Times* called his immigration policy the best of all candidates.

"Where's Megyn?" shouts a man, irritating a woman I assume is his wife.

Ed points his automatic zapper and Megyn reappears. Ted Cruz grins like a shy freshman getting stroked by the junior prom queen. And Megyn, feeling some of the senator's new star power, gradually becomes more deferential.

"Back to Hillary and Bernie," orders a female.

Stoic Hillary is told a *Washington Post* poll reveals only thirty-seven percent of those questioned think she's honest. She says she doesn't think that's fair or founded, and after all she's been on the hot seat a quarter of a century, but she takes responsibility and is confident people see she's fighting for them.

Bernie, grasping for glory, which will disappear if he loses Florida and Ohio next week, says Hillary should release transcripts of her private speeches to Wall Street corporations. After all, stresses Bernie, she got two hundred twenty-five grand each time so these must be great speeches and she should share utterances of that quality. Furthermore, Bernie says Wall Street has provided fifteen million to Super PACs representing Hillary, and the campaign finance system is broken.

Jorge Ramos, a few months ago ejected from a rally for pressuring Trump about immigration, asks Hillary if she lied to families of victims in Benghazi. Hillary responds no and that she so testified before Congress for eleven hours. Bernie stresses he's not going to discuss Benghazi but rebukes Hillary for supporting the ouster of Colonel Muammar Gaddafi. Bernie doesn't like forcing regime changes.

"Check what's on Fox," a man demands.

Donald Trump is talking to Sean Hannity. Bernie and Hillary are good performers, but more in the style of supporting actors. The Donald's charisma envelops us and no one complains about listening to his typical boasts and complaints. It doesn't matter what he says. He's therefore able to again tell us he was a great student who went to the best schools and is a very nice guy who only attacks opponents when they attack him. I swear he said this without laughing: "People attack me, like Jeb Bush, then they're gone."

We leave victorious Donald to hear Maria Elena Salinas, who's teamed with Jorge Ramos since Ronald Reagan resided in the White House, ask Hillary if she understands the needs of Latinos. Naturally, she says she does and plans to raise the minimum wage and make sure women receive equal pay for equal work. Bernie'll outdo that. He'll raise the minimum wage to fifteen bucks an hour and rebuild the nation's infrastructure.

"Why do so many poor whites support Republicans?" asks a woman.

That's a mystery. There's nothing unclear to Hillary about the Affordable Care Act – the wonderful or infamous Obamacare. She emphasizes ninety percent of the people are now covered and the smart approach is to build on that and reduce the cost. Bernie bemoans current high deductibles and the exorbitant cost of drugs.

Two dozen Florida mayors, fearful their descendents will have to flee an ever-rising sea, want to ask the candidates about climate change. They should be asking Donald Trump, who says sure, weather changes, but it's not because of people, weather just changes hot to cold, cold to hot. In the fall the probable candidates, Hillary and The Donald, will frequently joust over this issue. Tonight Hillary says climate change is clearly man-made. Bernie says we're looking at the senator who introduced the most comprehensive climate change legislation.

The topic changes to Latin America and Cuba, cherished bogeyman of the United States. Hillary says the Cuban people deserve freedom and democracy and that the Castro brothers weren't elected and, by inference, won't yield dictatorial power until they die. We're shown a 1985 clip of Bernie praising Fidel for educating Cuban kids and providing excellent health care. Some in the Miami crowd hiss. Bernie's ready, noting the eternal embargo has to end and full diplomatic relations would be good for the Cuban people. I've recently read many young Cuban Americans in Florida, unlike their forefathers and hawkish Marco Rubio, also feel that way.

Ed switches back to Fox. Damn, The Donald's gone, but Megyn Kelly's back, talking to Rubio. Too bad Trump and Megyn squabbled and he said something about one of her orifices. She'd have made a great vice presidential running mate. I'm not kidding. Besides, the alternative is Ted Cruz.

Is Trump the Moderate Republican?

Donald Trump, a racist, fear-mongering xenophobe, continues to paradoxically show some philosophical flexibility as he kicks the electoral asses of three hidebound career politicians – Ted Cruz, Marco Rubio, and John Kasich – who, even as they march toward presidential irrelevance, cling by their teeth to failed Cold War rhetoric and doctrines that were outdated, though popular, a half century ago. Being a Cold Warrior today isn't wise, but neither are the belligerent people who dominate both political parties. Trump again capitalized on this during the debate in Coral Gables.

This reserved praise for Donald Trump, as foreign policy strategist, should not deflect attention from his refusal to disavow or modify his claim that one point six billion Muslims hate us. All of them, he was asked? Well, a lot of them, said The Donald. And what about his desire to "take out" families of terrorists? Trump asserted we have to expand laws, especially regarding torture, or we're a "bunch of suckers." Rubio and Cruz piously disagreed.

Yet, in most matters overseas, Donald Trump is the moderate, and Cruz, Rubio, and Kasich are warmongers. Rather than let the United States continue as the blindered-lapdog of Israel, Trump emphasized it's "important for Palestinians to believe a deal can get done." Rubio, pockets stuffed with Super PAC money from only-Israel-counts donors like Sheldon Adelson and Paul Singer, repeated his inevitable spiel that the Palestinian Authority is not interested in a peace deal; it only wants to attack Israel (and, evidently, suffer many times more casualties than Israel.) The south Florida crowd applauded Rubio but silently received Trump's John-Lennon-like response that he wants to "give peace a chance." Republicans don't like peace. They need war and economic catastrophe so they can be perpetually angry and trigger more wars and recessions. John Kasich, who several weeks ago said the United States needs to "punch Russia" in the snout – will big bad John personally deliver the punch and deal with the counterpunch?

– continued his saber rattling, stating there is "no long-term peace" opportunity in Israel and Palestine. How the hell does John Kasich know? One should also note that Rubio doesn't seem to have the words West Bank or Palestine in his lexicon; the highly-paid sycophant calls that area Judea and Samaria.

Tough Ted Cruz tried to out-Trump Trump regarding Mexico, promising to build a wall, triple the border patrol, end sanctuary cities, and cut off welfare for those without documentation. Canadian-born Cruz is also anxious, from day one of his presidency, to eliminate the Iran nuclear treaty, vaporize Obamacare, and axe the department of education.

Hand Marco Rubio a globe and he'd have trouble identifying any areas he doesn't want to attack or at least bully. He believes the Chinese need to be disciplined in the South China Sea, which Rubio considers an American lake. As noted, he's ready to slit more Palestinian throats to please his pro-Israel puppeteers. Naturally, he wants to destroy ISIS. Even Bernie Sanders wants to do that. But how? With American "boots," the quaint euphemism that doesn't say people are in those boots. And after ISIS is "destroyed," like the Taliban in 2002, what then? Permanent American boots on the ground, perhaps.

Rubio passionately opposes President Obama's upcoming trip to Cuba, the land Rubio's future parents abandoned two years before Fidel Castro took power. He'd wanted you to assume they were refugees but word got out. No problem. Rubio received the loudest hand of the night when he denounced Cuba for being undemocratic and harboring criminals and thieves. If so, they're like decades of close friends of the United States.

What does Donald Trump think about Cuba? He feels fifty-five years of unnecessary enmity are quite enough and it's time to start making deals.

Those seeking a Republican presidential candidate who isn't danger-ous won't find one. Democratic shoo-in Hillary Clinton is also a Cold Warrior seeking to prove something – perhaps the psychic presence of gonads – by starting a war, and preferably more than one.

I could never vote for Donald Trump. But I can envision him negotiating more and shooting less than Hillary Clinton, Ted Cruz,

Marco Rubio, or John Kasich. The least belligerent candidate, Bernie Sanders, has no chance. He's a pinko socialist who wants poor people and the middle class to have more money and the superrich to have less. At least Rubio and Kasich also are out of it in all respects except blowing hot air. Trump's got too many enemies to win, likewise way-right Cruz. So the presidency will probably be Hillary's, and there'll be times she's ordering attacks when Donald Trump would've tried to make a deal.

Cruz to the Moon

Friends, on this great Super Tuesday Two, I have again routed Donald Trump all over this great nation and, after starting the day some ninety delegates behind, now trail by a mere two hundred fifty. Don't be fooled by the math. In Florida I only lost by sixteen percent and ninety-nine delegates to none. I did even better in Illinois, compiling eight percent less than The Donald and spotting him twenty-four delegates to nada. In North Carolina I came within three percent and three delegates. And I almost won Missouri, needing only a few more votes. I didn't actually win Ohio, either, but neither did Trump. John Kasich took his home state and sixty-six delegates. Dreary John should go home and urge those delegates to back me, for only I, soaring Ted Cruz, can save the Republicans from Donald Trump, the one person on earth Hillary Clinton would defeat in November.

FIFTEEN

President Paul Ryan

Damn, I feel good. I'm a lucky guy. Blessed by God and spurred by hard work, I was elected to the House of Representatives at age twenty-eight and have biannually blown away all opponents since. You probably remember I ran for vice president on Mitt Romney's ticket four years ago. I think in a democracy if you want to be president you should go through the rigors of running for that office. That's why at this moment I'm not interested in being president. I enjoy serving as speaker of the house. I know I said I didn't want that job but was already in the building, and the first guy in line, Kevin McCarthy, really didn't want the job and almost everyone asked me to take it, so I did. That's different.

Now people are asking what I'll do if, as likely, Donald Trump doesn't have a majority of the delegates when we have our Republican convention this summer. Would I help them dump Trump after a ballot or two? Would I step in to save the country from a bumbling bigmouth who'd damage our party while losing to the egregious Hillary Clinton? My predecessor, John Boehner, said if no one wins on the first ballot, he's "for none of the above," and would support me. I haven't even been thinking about this stuff. Some don't believe any house speaker, who would lead the shaping of rules for delegates in a deadlocked convention, could avoid thinking about the presidency, but I don't think I'm interested.

Really, I know I'm pretty sure I'm where I should be. I like the view. Did you see me sitting behind Barack Obama at his final State of the Union speech in January? I didn't clap much but sure looked grim, just as I'd practiced in front of my mirror in the Capitol. That's where I live. I don't have an apartment in Washington, D.C. I work late and focus on legislation and my family back in Wisconsin and don't have time to do much else but rip Trump for failing to denounce David Duke and the KKK, for seeking to ban Muslim immigrants, for not controlling his violent supporters at rallies, and now for threatening there'll be riots if at the convention he's denied the nomination.

I get up early and work out to cleanse my mind. I do the dynamic P90X program that includes yoga and chin-ups and lifting dumbbells and stretching and cardio exercises. Maybe I'll also run another meditative marathon. I once broke three hours in the event. Some muckrakers tried to look that up but couldn't confirm the performance. Really, I might've just said three hours because that's a pretty good time. Then someone claimed to have discovered my only official marathon time was about four hours. Who knows?

Pfizer's Little Pills

what'sa matter
bernie a little
grouchy today

i'll tell you

what

pfizer gouges
customers here
seeking merger
in ireland to
evade billions
in taxes

Cruz's Doomsday Strategies

Friends, my inept enemy in the race for the Republican nomination is, as you know, a despicable coward who refuses to debate me one on one. I suspect he's paying dreary John Kasich to stay in the race, to serve as his beard so he, The Donald, won't have to fight me like a man. That strategy has thus far worked but won't much longer. I'm going to change the equation – I'm currently trailing by a scant two hundred seventy-four delegates – by brilliantly capitalizing on my landslide victory last night in Utah where I tromped Trump sixty-nine percent to fourteen. Even Kasich beat him there. It doesn't matter Trump won more delegates by taking Arizona or that he's captured nineteen of twenty-nine primary elections.

This is what matters: Mormons love me. So do many other people but these folks out on the salt flats realize Donald Trump is a godless fraud and that I'm a religious and scholarly man who can save our country. What I've already started to do is say yes to thousands of Utah Mormons who want to serve in my campaign. They're in fact already packing to go to Wisconsin, Colorado, New York, Pennsylvania, California, and all other undecided states and talk to voters not merely about politics but promptly becoming Mormons so they, too, can better understand the nature of my candidacy. And when thousands of newly-proselytized Mormons soon become hundreds of thousands and then millions they can sweep the nation and ensure my victory if not by majority before the convention then certainly generate the political energy I need to prevail when I court delegates in backrooms.

There are other essential changes in my grand strategy. In the wake of the slaughter in Brussels, self-professed security enforcer Trump is again calling for torture of Islamic terrorists. I'm even tougher on this issue. As a young man sleek and strong, I will personally torture the terrorists. You know Trump's too aged to inflict much pain. I'm ready to grab their gonads before I waterboard them. I've also demanded that we police Muslim neighborhoods in this country to intimidate potential enemies and gather intelligence. We don't have nearly as many large, Muslim-majority 'hoods as the effete Europeans, and need to make sure we never do. President Ted Cruz knows how.

So far I've been restrained and gentlemanly, two of my many admirable qualities, about the fact that Melania – Trump's third wife (has he had only three?) – was a naked model for years and, one assumes, a courtesan as well. Nevertheless, I didn't post those photos of her. Thousands of moral citizens did that, and millions have seen her raw flesh. Trump tweeted I better be careful or he'll tweet the truth about my wife Heidi. I tweeted he's an even bigger coward than I thought. What could he have been referring to, anyway?

Bernie at Clooney's

bernie and
wife liquidate
everything
raising seven
hundred grand
to buy prime
tickets for
hillary event
at george
clooney's

Hillary's Prediction

sure
i lost
washington
alaska and
hawaii but
up come
new york and
pennsylvania
and down
goes bernie

Bernie Beckons

hillary
can't
you
hear
my
calls
for
a
new
york
debate

Lectern

at
empty
lectern
bernie
awaits
queen
of
war
and
wall
street

SIXTEEN

Pro Trump

i was very
pro choice
now i'm not
i'm warning
all bimbo
pigs they'll
be punished
if they disobey
after I outlaw
abortions

Reince Priebus Mobilizes

It is, in a general political and philosophical sense, unforgivable that I don't already enjoy a hundred percent name recognition among the American people and, indeed, all people in the civilized world. I have nevertheless decided to forgive everyone, except myself, since it's my duty alone to emblazon the name of Reince Priebus across the political firmament. This glorious task I today undertake in my Wisconsin bunker where I've summoned Paul Ryan and my amanuensis, Governor Scott Walker.

"It's time to do something about Donald Trump," I say.

"I could reenter the race," says Walker.

"The public, when it noticed, perceived you as a union-battering reactionary. As chairman of the Republican National Committee, I've been reaching out to other races and genders and growing the party. Take notes, Scott, nothing more."

"I sense you're alluding to my becoming president at our contested convention this summer," says Ryan.

"I'm afraid that's a senseless remark. You're viewed as a far right loon who, with Mitt Romney, blundered into Obama's quicksand of 2012. The Grand Old Party needs a dynamic candidate who carries a splendid record."

"If not I, then who?"

"Reince Priebus, my foolish friend."

"Reince," Ryan says, "in 2004 you couldn't even get elected to the state senate."

"I've since run the table just as I had before. Let me remind both of you, as I shall tonight inform the American people on all radio and TV stations: I served as student body president in college, and during law school I not merely became president of all law school students, I clerked in various courts and assisted the NAACP. You mention my inconsequential loss in 2004 but conveniently omit my victory two years later, and the 2007 tidal wave leading to my chairmanship of the Republican Party in Wisconsin. Gentlemen, you surely know that Reince Priebus was merely limbering up. My organizational skills and strategic insight in 2011 enabled us to obliterate the Democratic machine that had so long burdened our great state.

"The following year, a seminal one for the GOP, I won another election – a national election, where you've both failed – and have since twice been reelected by landslides as chairman of the burgeoning RNC. I'm already a legend, albeit in too few places, for slashing debt and raising revenues and enhancing our technological communications with the American people, even including minorities and women, who will cherish our values once I've clarified what they are."

"Frankly, Reince, you don't have the star power to become president," says Ryan. "You're simply the Karl Rove of your generation."

"And you're our John Boehner, speaker of the house never to further rise. When voters understand my superlative record, they'll abandon Trump and Ted Cruz and join the Reince Priebus vanguard."

"We better plan our new strategy for the convention," says Walker.

"Yes, and that strategy begins with my sledgehammer victory in our Wisconsin primary next week and in all subsequent primaries certain to generate an overwhelming advantage for Reince Priebus in polls against Hillary Clinton."

"Will you please consider me as your running mate?" Ryan asks.

"We can't have two guys from Wisconsin and especially the same vice presidential candidate twice in a row."

"Who then?" asks Ryan.

"Governor Nikki Haley of South Carolina."

"She may have personal issues."

"Not with me."

Trump Erupts in Wisconsin

I better not speak tonight. In Wisconsin Governor Scott Walker just ganged up with other inept politicians, pundits, and donors and tried to stop my revolution to save America. Their fake victory is actually quite modest, forty-eight percent to thirty-five, and thirty-three delegates to three. Big deal. I still lead Lyin' Ted Cruz by more than two hundred delegates.

And in two weeks New York and its ninety-five delegates are coming. Will Cruz admit I'm leading him by about thirty-four percent there? Will he tell you in winner-take-all Pennsylvania and Maryland I'm ahead by seventeen and nine points, respectively, and figure to earn a hundred nine delegates just from those two states? No, he won't but voters will.

Backroom pols don't get it: people are demanding someone different.

Math Teacher Scolds Bernie

Dear Bernie,

Hi, there. Remember me? This is Miss Smith, your third grade math teacher from Brooklyn. I bet you're surprised I'm still alive. I just turned ninety-nine last week. I live in a home for old folks and many of us gather to watch all the debates and everyone thinks it's wonderful you were my student.

"Was he good at math?" they often ask.

"No, he was bad then, too. Almost had to flunk him."

I'm not writing to criticize you, Bernie. We need a different kind of politician who wants all citizens to share in our nation's wealth. I'm voting for you in the New York primary in a couple of weeks. But I wanted you to know the email you sent after winning in Wisconsin concerns me. You wrote, "We are on the path to the Democratic nomination for president."

I just wish that was true. Please let your old teacher explain why it isn't. First, you trail Hillary Clinton by about two hundred fifty delegates. Your big win in Wisconsin only gained you nine more delegates than Hillary received. And I'm worried about our huge home state of New York. She leads you by around eleven percent in the polls. I think she's going to win here, Bernie. And there's certainly no way for you to pick up many more delegates than she, even if you close like gangbusters and win a white-knuckler. Then there's Pennsylvania where you're trailing by eighteen percent and Maryland where you're behind by twenty-eight. You're going to fall further behind, and in early June comes California where she's up by ten. Even if you blaze to the finish line, you won't be able to cut much of her lead. And we should admit Hillary's ahead in popular votes by more than two million.

The numbers just don't work, Bernie. I'm attaching some elementary addition and subtraction problems, and I want you to solve them and send me the answers.

You're doing a great job making Hillary and the voters think about things from a different perspective.

Sincerely,

Miss Elvira Jones

Hillary and Bernie at the Laundromat

I was at a Bronx laundromat last night, bemoaning my inability to rent an apartment large enough to accommodate a washer and dryer and fearing this would forever be my fate, when in trudged Bernie Sanders, bearing a big basket of dirty clothes.

"Senator, you've got my support," I said. "But what are you doing in a joint like this?"

"I'm the only working class candidate in this presidential race. Every day I struggle to get by."

"Your campaign brought in forty-five million bucks last month."

"That money belongs to the people. I'd never touch a cent."

He turned to the washers and tossed pants into one, shirts in another, and everything else into the third.

"Bernie, you're trailing by about eleven percent in New York and the election's in less than two weeks."

"No problem. I'm accustomed, as in Wisconsin, to trailing by fifty points, then forty, then on down to ten before the election, and then I win. I've won seven of the last eight primaries, you know."

"Yeah, but except for Michigan those are primarily white states. You've lost, and lost big, where there are lots of blacks and Hispanics. New York, Pennsylvania, and California are certainly diverse places."

"That's to my advantage, despite previous results. Minorities are learning I'm far more attuned to their concerns than my opponent."

"Unbelievable…"

"How so?"

"Look," I said, pointing to the door through which Hillary Clinton backed as she balanced a heaping laundry basket on her head.

"Amazed you're here, Bernie," she said. "I thought some of your millions of volunteers and donors, greased by new money, would be handling all your chores."

"Hillary, your presence here is a farce and an affront to the working people of this nation. You must be keeping me under surveillance."

"No need for that. I'm just saving money because we can't match your fundraising."

"And most unfortunate for you, since we're now face to face and you can no longer deny me a New York debate."

Bernie points to me and says, "Record this on your cell phone. I want working people to hear me tell Hillary she's unqualified to be president of the United States. You, madam, take money from megabanks and super PACs while helping fat cats avoid paying taxes. You belong in a Wall Street suite, not in the Oval Office."

"Bernie, your tired repetitions of the same theme convince me you're not really a Democrat. You advocate unlimited rights and impunity for gun manufacturers, no matter what carnage is wreaked by their weapons. That puts you to the right of many Republicans. And your incoherent – should I say communistic – cries to break up the big banks underscore how little you've actually pondered these issues. Frankly, you don't know squat about real economic policies."

"That's your narrative, Hillary, and it's sent you on an extended losing streak."

"We're back on my urban turf, Bernie. Get ready for the rout."

"I'm ready to keep reminding people that while you're hustling money from the wealthiest I'm scurrying to help the middle class and poor. They're disgusted by your claims I can't win. I can win. People know you voted to authorize the criminal invasion of Iraq in 2003. Americans don't want money-grabbing warmongers."

"What the people don't want is an aging, and perhaps senile, ideologue who hasn't done his political and financial homework. You're so obsessed with being Saint Bernie the Savior that you've ignored the real challenges of running a nation."

"There would be no positive changes in a Hillary Clinton administration."

"You're getting awfully grumpy and will become more so after New York. But don't worry. I have a present for you."

From her basket Hillary pulled a T-shirt that across the front announced:

Love

trumps

Hate

Battle of Brooklyn

Thousands of tough New York fight fans crowd into a smoky Brooklyn arena and begin cheering, hissing, clapping, and booing long before the fighters appear in the ring, which actually is a stage without ropes. Technicalities don't matter. Bernie Sanders enters ready to rumble, ripping a hook to the body as he demands Hillary Clinton release transcripts from her Wall Street speeches, for which she received mighty big bucks. Sure, counters Hillary, she'll do that, if everyone else in the race does, too. One wonders what she said to her generous listeners.

Angered by Bernie's jealously of her friendships with the wealthy, she blasts him for the greed and recklessness of gun manufactures who Bernie has comforted for a quarter century, promising the NRA he would oppose waiting periods for gun buyers and five times voting against the gun-wary Brady Bill. Bernie says he was protecting small businesses, the gun shops which should not be liable when crimes are committed with weapons they legally sold; those who sell illegally should be responsible. Invoking his name in the third person, he says decades ago Bernie Sanders was against assault weapons.

Moving in as he absorbs Hillary's hammers, Bernie right crosses that as secretary of state she worked hard to expand fracking all over the world. Partially deflecting the blow with a forearm, Hillary hooks that as president she'll install a half billion solar panels and notes she supports clean renewable energy. We must transition away from fossil fuels, Bernie insists.

Gangs of supporters throughout the arena stand to exhort their candidate and deride the opponent, producing delightful Bronx cheers and generating energy in what had become, in both parties, a dreary and predictable series of preliminary fights. Tonight Bernie rushes Hillary, lambasting her for being the strongest supporter of what President Obama says was the worst mistake of his administration: attacking Libya but not preparing for life after Muammar Gaddafi. Further, rumbles Bernie, Hillary was a chest-beating advocate of attacking Iraq in 2003 and unaware that regime changes often bring unintended consequences. Hillary nails Bernie's forehead, asserting that problems are greater in Syria because we didn't remove Bashar al-Assad. Bernie counters he's against a no fly zone and advocates destroying ISIS first, and then Assad. Hillary insists we need safe havens for Syrians fleeing both ISIS and Assad. Thousands of fans demand a fight between Assad and Abu Bakr al-Baghdadi, leader of ISIS.

Bernie taunts Hillary that we provide seventy-five percent of NATO's resources, and should insist wealthy nations like Germany, France, and England quit riding us and pay their share. Field Marshal Hillary, who seems to crave war, pounds Bernie's jaw that NATO is the most successful military alliance in human history. Let us surmise that heroic Hillary plans to personally patrol the Russian front, cradling her purse laden with nuclear codes.

In the city with more Jews than any in the world, Bernie stresses Israel has the right to defend itself, and he understands this because as a child he spent many months there, but in Gaza his brethren have responded disproportionately to Palestinian attacks and relentlessly bombed civilian areas, and someday the United States is going to have to treat the Palestinians with respect. Appalled at accusations of Israeli excess, two-fisted Hillary bellows that as secretary of state she negotiated the 2012 ceasefire in Gaza. Ducking her blows, Bernie again states the Israeli response was disproportionate and there will never be peace until the United States plays an evenhanded role.

Moving inside, Bernie plants himself and says we're the only major country on earth without universal health care, and our colleges are too damned expensive. Hillary, circling away, concedes we have to make college and health care affordable but must be sure medical figures add up. Vermont-dwelling Bernie wonders why his neighbor Canada makes the figures work but we can't. Canada's not a communist country and is doing okay, he notes.

Hillary's the more stylish pugilist but brawling Bernie excites fans as he scores that his millions of dollars come from an average donation of twenty-seven dollars, unlike Wall Street windfalls for Hillary, who left hooks Bernie's ribs that she's received two-point-three million more votes than he.

Right, says Bernie, we got murdered in the Deep South, invoking images of slain civil rights activists from the sixties. Hillary enumerates her many wins and delegate lead of two hundred fifty.

In the final round Bernie says he's Brooklyn born and the son of a Polish immigrant who never had much, and he disagrees you can get money from Wall Street, PACs, and special interests and still do what working people need.

Hillary thanks the people of New York for twice giving her the honor of serving as their senator. They took on 9/11 together and she knows New Yorkers appreciate she's always fighting barriers economic, racial, and gender-related. She doesn't just make promises, she'll deliver results.

Each candidate raises both hands and walks around the ring, nodding at supporters and waiting for judgment at the New York primary next week.

Bernie Cruz

"Bernie, guess you heard I got fifteen percent and no delegates in New York and trail Trump by less than three hundred and am positioned to win on the second ballot at the convention."

"Me too, Ted, I won forty-two percent and only lost by thirty-one delegates who know Hillary's superdelegates are bound to come to me."

"Look at polls proving I'm even with Hillary in the fall and Trump trails her by nine."

"Don't forget, Ted, polls say I'd beat you by ten and Trump by sixteen."

"That would probably change. Anyway, it's certain we're the two strongest candidates."

"That's why I know my working class backers will understand convention bullshit's more important than their votes."

"If we can't steal the nominations, let's form an independent Cruz-Sanders ticket."

"Sanders-Cruz."

SEVENTEEN

Cruz Trumped

trump
takes
all
counties
five
states
while
cruz
kisses
carly

Gracious Donald

I'm so proud of Ted Cruz. He's a competitive guy and just a wonderful man, and his wife Heidi's a marvelous woman, and hot, too. Let me tell you, I'd do Heidi if I weren't running for president. I know I called Ted a liar and basket case during a debate and later christened him Lyin' Ted. That's just politics. I'm super competitive: sports, business, babes, whatever I want, I compete for. And I win. America never wins anymore, but that'll change when I become president, and few doubt I'll be in the White House now that I've kicked Cruz and John Kasich out of Indiana and the Republican primary. It's my time to transform America into a great big beautiful loving country.

I'm a loving guy. Look at my family. They're always here supporting me. Notice how I've positioned them tonight, gorgeous Melania to my left, stunning Ivanka to my right, and comely Vanessa, one of my two incredible daughters in law, behind me. Name one presidential candidate in our history who's had this kind of family beauty. I'm not going to brag too much. My people tell me I don't have to, everyone'll notice. That's good advice. I'm trying to be more presidential and, frankly, that's not hard because I'm born to lead.

I want to run a clean campaign and will unless haggy Hillary tries to trash me. I don't want to have to remind you that her husband's a lecherous boor. Yeah, I know, some people have called me that, too. But I'm slick as Slick Willie, and Hillary isn't, so when mud starts flying I'll be bobbing and weaving while she takes the hits.

I'd advise Hillary to be ladylike when she sends her emails. As I celebrated our nation's nomination of me, Hillary was complaining I still plan to build a huge wall on the Mexican border, and jail women who have abortions after I change the law, and bar Muslims from entering our loving country. Yes, I'm going to build the wall. No, women won't be jailed, probably just fined for breaking anti-abortion laws I'll make sure are passed. And what does she want me to do about Muslims? Invite ISIS in? Listen, I doubt Hillary will even be the

Democrat running against me. She'll be in jail. Either way, Donald Trump is your next president.

Trump the Kremlinologist

cia debriefed
the donald
about russian
nukes politics
and economics
after his big
incredible miss
universe contest

Hello Donald

as a young
woman i met
donald trump
and extended
my hand but
he stepped
inside to
kiss my
mouth

Trump Embraces Guns

Thank God for the NRA, a group of patriots who, led by me as president, will save America from Hillary Clinton and her tyrannical desire to destroy the second amendment. Don't believe her denials; she intends to do so. Don't pay attention to those who claim four years ago I praised President Obama for advocating tighter gun laws after another public slaughter, this one at an elementary school in Newtown, Connecticut; that's liberal distortion. Remember: I'm no longer a liberal. I never really was. I just sounded like one.

I'm certainly not a liberal today, addressing NRA members who get excited when I tell them my sons have so many guns even I get worried. I'm not really worried, of course. I love it when law-abiding people have guns. We've got to have guns and lots of them. Three hundred million in this country aren't enough. Other countries need to arm themselves much better. If the good guys had had guns in Paris, far fewer concert goers would have been killed.

We're not going to have any more massacres like in Paris and Newtown because we're getting rid of gun free zones. Teachers, administrators, and security guards must all be armed. Music lovers should also be packing. People need guns, yet Hillary wants to disarm citizens in high crime neighborhoods. She aims to make them vulnerable while she releases violent criminals from prisons across the nation. She doesn't want there to be thirteen million holders of concealed weapons permits. That's too bad. I'm one of those permit holders and, if I weren't surrounded by secret service agents, I'd be blowing away bad guys all the time.

Bubba Does Kern County

I don't know why I arrive an hour early to hear Bill Clinton speak at the United Farms Workers convention in Bakersfield. I shouldn't have even arrived on time for the two p.m. speech. I know Bubba's always late. At two-thirty-six UFW president Arturo Rodriguez announces, "He's on his way." That means the former president is far away and slowly approaching. He's probably pressing flesh or having his hair cut by a Hollywood sculptor on the tarmac of LAX, as he did in 1993. I remember being angry at the time, but later learned rumors the executive trim delayed commercial traffic were inaccurate, though not retracted by newspapers reporting the story.

Bill Clinton wouldn't mess with aviation but he'll make you wait in an auditorium. About three o'clock I consider leaving but don't because I want to see a man fill an arena with his personality, and keep listening to good speakers, waiting for a great one. At last we're told he's here. It's three-thirty-five and a tall man with elegantly coiffed gray hair and an almost-matching blazer steps on stage, enlivening the room as he's greeted by smiling faces. Dolores Huerta, an octogenarian who helped Cesar Chavez found the UFW, is one of those granted closeness.

Clinton says he'll be brief – when has that happened? – and the crowd groans, prompting the born communicator to say, "Not that brief." He notes that borders the world over are being erased and economies damaged and we wonder if we can create security for everyone. The Republicans want to deport people and build barriers and pay people less. Shall we close our borders or open our hearts, Clinton asks a crowd almost entirely Hispanic. When we turn away from people and say they're less than we are, just to get votes, he implies we're acting like the other party and stresses Hillary wants everyone to grow and work together.

We need comprehensive immigration reform with a path to citizenship, he says. The other guy's idea for a wall across our Mexican border is a bad choice for America's future. We don't need a wall. We need equal rights for women and a release of nonviolent prisoners who've been in jail too long. We must ask if it's wise to keep people angry all the time. Do we want walls or do we want bridges? Does America stand for we or me? The other guy thinks it's all about him, Clinton says; his wife, by contrast, has spent a lifetime enabling people and fighting to end discrimination and get overtime all workers including the United Farm Workers.

Clinton finishes speaking after twenty minutes, having held a personal conversation with most of those present. He believes what he says, and yearns for a return to power even if only as influential husband of the next commander in chief.

EIGHTEEN

Trump Counters Foreign Policy Speech

Okay, I'll take a few minutes to respond to Crooked Hillary's lies about my positions on foreign policy. I didn't actually watch her phony speech. I tried but she put me to sleep. She should forget politics and ride her broomstick around selling medications for insomnia. That'll keep her busy until she goes to jail for fraudulent use of emails while bombing as secretary of state.

Don't forget, folks, I'm the one who didn't want to go to Iraq. How can Hillary accuse me of trying to scare Americans when as senator she schemed to make you think Saddam Hussein had nuclear weapons? Now she's accusing me of saying all sorts of things I don't remember saying or that I wish I hadn't said or that were taken out of context. And based on these phantom statements, which at most were political punches, she called me dangerously incoherent as well as unprepared and temperamentally unfit to be president. Let me tell you what I think you already know: I'm tough as hell temperamentally, so much tougher than Hillary ever could be. Yet, she claimed I'm so thin skinned I'd blunder us into a war. She in fact knows when I'm president everyone will be so afraid of us that I won't have to order a war.

I don't want to give Hillary's lies too much coverage but I'll deal with some of them. She accused me of wanting nuclear weapons for more countries and threatening to abandon our NATO allies and planning to torture and murder relatives of those accused of torture. I really don't know what I think about nuclear weapons because they never came up at real estate meetings or beauty pageants. I never said we should abandon NATO, I just said those rich European countries should pay their share. That's fair. Regarding torture, I'm telling our terrorist enemies, and that means Muslims, don't mess with President Trump. Got it?

I didn't literally mean the United States is weak militarily, as she accused me of believing. We have the greatest soldiers in the world and I guarantee lots of generals want me to be their commander in chief because they know I'll be bold and exciting. What I really meant was that black President Obama is a weakling and has made people around the world laugh at us and believe we're weak. Trust me, no one would dare laugh at an America led by powerful President Trump.

Hillary wants you to believe I'd have this country cowering behind walls, my defensive barrier along our Mexican border. We wouldn't cower. We'd be safe and relaxed, like when I'm surrounded by guards in Trump Tower. She also claimed I'd ruin our alliances by picking fights with friends. Listen, if they're friends, they'll do what I say. Then it'll be easier to destroy ISIS and control North Korea, whose leader Kim Jong-Un I've usually condemned rather than praised. I can't remember making the remark that Japan and North Korea, if they have a nuclear war, should just enjoy themselves. That sounds like one of Hillary's deleted emails. She also attacked me for being against our nuclear deal with Iran. It feels good to protest that the deal doesn't prevent the Iranians from getting nukes. The deal doesn't matter, anyway, because I'll never let the Iranians have those weapons.

I could go on but won't. I'd be asleep and you probably already are. When you wake up, remember this: I've gotten more primary votes than any Republican ever has. And another thing Hillary hopes you won't find out: blacks, Latinos, and Muslims love me.

Trump Subtle in Victory

Tonight I'm not going to talk about the mysterious deaths of Antonin Scalia and Vince Foster, or the perplexing birth of Barack Obama, or an Indiana-Mexican judge unfairly attacking me about superlative Trump University, or about walls on our borders. Having just finished the Republican primary as overwhelming winner, I'm going to speak about the need to care for our long-mistreated African Americans, and how to protect our workers from foreign predators, and my pledge never to fight any war unless it makes us safer, and, most importantly, my determination to save the nation from more problems caused by hedge-fund Hillary.

Trump Delight

perceptive
candidate
says
many
congratulate
him
after
orlando
nightclub
massacre

Banished by Trump

all muslims
are after us
especially obama
who must resign
immediately and
sit in corner with
washington post

Senatorial Guns

senate sucks
guns delighting
nra nanny
which feeds
automatic
weapons to
the deranged

Campaign Finance

thought
the donald
was gonna
write his
campaign
big checks
instead he's
emailin' me
for dough

Trump Store

cruz was only lying
ted now i have to beat
lying crooked hillary
at grand trump store
where only fifty
bucks gets you trump
campaign button official
trump make america great
again bumper sticker
trump window cling and
trump sticker

NINETEEN

Vice President Mike Pence

Hi, let me introduce myself to the ninety-eight percent of you who've never heard of me. I'm Mike Pence, governor of Indiana and a former six-term congressman. I love God and hate big government which forces businessmen to sell their services to homosexuals who want to get married, and allows women and their doctors to kill unborn babies, and believes in passing out clean needles to drug addicts who don't get any help in Indiana until AIDS is rampant in their county. I know when government's getting too liberal and dangerous, and in 2001 wrote a column lambasting Congress for pretending tobacco's a killer. "In fact, two out of every three smokers don't die from a smoking related illness and nine of ten smokers don't contract lung cancer." I'm not saying smoke. Don't smoke. But either way, that should be your choice. You've got to remember that "a government big enough to go after smokers is a government big enough to go after you." Donald Trump agrees.

Cruz Convention

donald kept
calling me
lyin' ted
so I stood
on convention
stage and
omitted his
ass

Picking the Right Trump

Republicans have endured a year of caustic campaigning by seventeen blowhards and selected the loudest mouth in the group, Donald Trump, who aroused his troops at the Republican National Convention with cries for more fear and anger. To hear Trump's version of life in this land, we should be buying more guns because of rampant crime and violence, preparing our tin cups to receive aid not forthcoming from a failed economy, calling the police to report the "terrible, terrible crimes" of Hillary Clinton who has brought so much "death, destruction, and terrorism" to this troubled planet, preparing to wage trade wars against China and Mexico and others who fleece us, mobilizing for a shooting war against the monolithic caliphate called ISIS, raising hammers and shovels to transform our southern border into a walled colossus, preparing handcuffs for the corporate brigands who seek to move businesses to other lands, sharpening our swords to dramatically cut taxes, bemoaning the agony wrought by Obamacare, and, most urgently, casting our votes for the only person on earth who can and will fight for America and win.

I'm sorry, but this man is just too hyperactive and deranged to be president. Yes, I know his opponent is herself quite imperfect, and I don't say she should be handed the office. What I propose, and what the armed forces of the United States have agreed to enforce, is the selection of the proper Trump to run for the presidency of this great nation. Wives one and three, Ivana and Melania, were born in alien lands and are thus ineligible. Precocious and sartorially splendid Barron, though a lad of immeasurable promise, is simply too young at age ten. Lively Tiffany, daughter of Marla Maples and the second youngest of five, is a fine student, an orator of note, and a gifted socializer, but at age twenty-two she, alas, is also ineligible. The same perhaps pigheaded constitutional rule – remember Alexander the Great conquered much in his twenties and died well before age thirty-five – also constrains dashing Eric Trump, age thirty-two, who exudes the stability and competence of a future leader. That leaves us with Ivanka, who'll turn the golden thirty-five in October, or her older brother Donald, Jr.

Either, clearly, would be more trustworthy than the bankruptcy-filing, epithet-firing paterfamilias. As I'm not undemocratic, I said let's vote. This opportunity I extended to the Joint Chiefs of Staff, our highest ranking military officers. They unanimously decreed, seven zip, to nominate Ivanka Trump as the Republican candidate. They praised young Don, noting he not merely looks like Frank Sinatra but also bears the strong pipes of Old Blue Eyes. He might still someday be nominated to run for the highest office. Now, though, we present the beautiful, blonde, and articulate Ivanka as the best the Republicans can today offer, and remind naysayers this young lady is a model and entrepreneur of renown, far more attuned to gender equality than her lecherous, sharp-tongued father, and offers poise and steadiness The Donald simply doesn't have. So we shall have our first female president, be she Hillary Clinton or Ivanka Trump. The latter believes that her father, whose hysterical response to this news necessitated his being sedated and confined to the maids' quarters in Trump Tower, will recover in time to campaign for her, and if he does he'd make a really great White House maintenance chief.

Trump Steps In

Okay, my commandos and I, disguised as immigrants and credentialed as delegates, make it inside the convention center in Philadelphia, and they look at me, eager eyes asking: when? I push both open hands down and say, "Easy, I'll let you know."

It's hard not to move right now. There's goofy Elizabeth Warren, who's always had her head in the public trough, disrespecting my unbelievable business career. She portrays me as selfish and incompetent and dishonest. I really should intervene immediately but, like the ultimate poker player, I know when to hold 'em.

Geezer Bernie Sanders is soon hunched over the podium – I hope he doesn't fall onto it – and for the billionth time claims one-tenth of one percent owns more than the bottom ninety percent, and that Wall Street thieves almost ruined this country before Barack Obama became dictator, and Hillary Clinton must become president, and that I don't support an increase of the starvation minimum wage and even want to lower it, and Sanders fantasizes Democrats will offer free college tuition at public universities if you come from a family earning a hundred twenty-five grand or less.

"Go," I order, and we charge onto stage where security guards detain us until I rip off my Grouch Marx nose and mustache.

"It's Trump…"

"Damn right," I say, and remove my work shirt to reveal a beautiful Trump University T-shirt, only $199.95. "Don't waste time on public universities that spawn losers and bureaucrats and other Democrats. Come to Trump University and learn the dynamic secrets to becoming a billionaire. Don't listen to slanderous statements made by those who never attended or bitter remarks by those too stupid to understand our curriculum. Besides, this time I'll personally be teaching all classes. Lucky students will listen to my lectures in person, others will see them live on closed circuit. I can do all that and still easily defeat lyin' Hillary Clinton, who'll probably be in jail before November, anyway.

Here, form lines in front of my troops and they'll sign you up. All we need are your credit cards and driver's licenses."

Hundreds of Democrats, already battered by blubbering Al Franken, Cory Booker, and Michelle Obama, rush to line up. I swear, even Bernie steps in line. Remember, the guy's still not even a millionaire.

"Okay, folks, while I start making these people really rich, let me also show you some bottles of our finest Trump Wines."

"You don't drink," a woman shouts.

"Right, I don't, but many people do, and with Trump Wines you'll always drink moderately."

We pass out thousands of bottles and Democrats start drinking.

"All right, don't be socialists. Be dynamic capitalists. Make things happen. Start businesses. Hire people. Earn lots of money. Keep creating. Have an incredible time. Here you go, eat these Trump Steaks." Security men I'd secretly hired rush in, pushing carts filled with the finest beef cooked just how you like it.

I'm thrilled until I notice a big screen over the stage still bears the picture of Bernie Sanders, who's already signed up for Trump U and is swigging wine.

"Get that picture outta there," I order, staring at the technicians. In seconds the screen's alive with beautiful images of my spectacular Trump Golf Courses around the nation and world. "These are the greatest and will only cost you two or three hundred dollars a round for the public layouts. Memberships at private courses aren't cheap but they're fair.

"If you're not up for golf, I've got gambling palaces for you in Las Vegas and Atlantic City. Don't worry which ones I own and which ones went bankrupt and all that stuff Democrats keep talking about. If it says Trump on the building, you're guaranteed a quality experience."

"But we're in Philadelphia," a man says.

"No problem. Trump Airlines can whisk you anywhere."

Obama at the Convention

I love being on a big stage, crooning I'm more optimistic about America than ever before and how well my administration handled the recession and eliminated Osama bin Laden and forged the Iran nuclear deal and normalized relations with Cuba and cut homelessness in half and created health care for millions who didn't have it. I've already seduced the spectators, and their enraptured faces soothe me as I continue this isn't our typical election. It's a more fundamental choice about who we are as a people. We aren't like those deeply pessimistic and hateful Republican conventioneers we saw in Cleveland. The America I know is decent and generous. And for the edification of Donald Trump, we understand that America is already strong, America is already great, and here comes Hillary Clinton, my supremely-qualified comrade who I embrace and together we ease around the stage, smiling and waving.

Afterward, I hold a press conference.

The Media – Do you still think you could win a third term if the Constitution permitted you to run?

Barack Obama – Yes, I do, and quite easily.

TM – Isn't that rather insulting to Secretary Clinton?

BO – Look, I beat her when I was a political beginner, in a global sense, and my achievements in office, combined with my oratory and charm, assure that I'd defeat her not by a split decision, as in 2008, but by a knockout.

TM – So you think you could also handle Trump?

BO – I'd thrash The Donald fifty-eight to forty-two, and would enjoy doing so.

TM – Are you also a supreme prognosticator? Who wins, Donald or Hillary?

BO – They're both burdened by character issues and unprecedented levels of unlikability, but for more than forty years Hillary's been a serious student of and activist in politics and international relations. The Donald, by contrast, is ignorant of every public policy issue one can name, and has devoted his life to gorging his wallet and fleecing others. Hillary's a public servant, as well as a Wall Street toady, but we can trust her, I think, far more than her opponent.

TM – Many have accused Hillary of being a warmonger. What's your response?

BO – She does like military action and even backed our apocalyptic 2003 invasion of Iraq, but that doesn't necessarily make her a warmonger.

TM – What does it make her?

BO – It still leaves her more qualified than her pathologically aggressive opponent.

I smile and wave no more questions and dance toward my secret service agents who lead me to my bestial limousine which rolls to Air Force One which floats me out of Philadelphia and back to the White House, a residence I'm not anxious to leave.

Madame Nominee

new hairstyle
nice suit
good makeup
decent speech
may win

Trump Polls

the
donald
fears
latest
polls
indicate
voter
fraud
in
november

Titanic Trump

hillary's
unhinged
unbalanced
destructive
and
will
worsen
as i plummet

TWENTY

Second Amendment Trump

don't
democrats
understand
gun-totin'
donald
wasn't
aiming
second
amendment
bullets
at
hillary
only
surefire
nra
activism

The Heritage Foundation Beckons Me

This very morning, at ten oh three, I received an exciting email invitation to become "part of an elite group of half a million Heritage Foundation members who believe in and fight to defend the Constitution and America's founding principles."

Once I donate fifty or a hundred dollars, I'll be authorized to carry my foundation "card with pride" as one who "will enable (their) essential work of guiding conservative leaders in Congress."

I checked to make sure the Heritage Foundation was okay and learned they're backing Donald Trump for president and tutoring him on the issues. The Donald used to be almost liberal but isn't anymore, so that's okay, and who cares that as a tax-exempt organization the foundation isn't really supposed to be directly involved in campaigns.

The president of the Heritage Foundation, Jim DeMint, former U.S. senator from South Carolina, is an intriguing fellow who before leaving office was renowned for being worth only forty thousand dollars, a total indicating he's either unusually honest or very foolish. Let's pray it could be the former since I'm worth even less than DeMint was. He's probably doing much better now and making a half million or so a year. Whether impoverished or affluent, Jim DeMint believes abortions should be illegal unless the mother's life is threatened, and he refuses to sanction same-sex marriage since such "behavior is considered immoral by all the world's religions."

By God, that's the information I needed. If I owned a house I'd mortgage it to hike Jim DeMint's salary.

Hillary Defends Clinton Foundation

Aren't those wonderful photos of Donald and Melania with Bill and me at their lavish Mar-a-Lago wedding a decade ago? The glamorous Trumps really like us, their smiles show, and we adore them, our expressions confirm, so I wonder why The Donald's making a big deal of the fact half the nongovernmental people I received as secretary of state had given or would give money to The Clinton Foundation. They didn't penetrate my inner sanctum because their donations averaged almost two million dollars. They got in on merit, because they had important business of government in their briefcases.

I know you've a hundred times heard hot-air Trump brag he knows all the important politicians in both parties and gives money to everyone and expects them to respond down the line when he asks favors. That's how business and life work. You stroke mine, I'll fondle yours. At least The Clinton Foundation battles poverty and disease around the world. Trump sought money only for himself. That's why I'll bust his balls in November.

El Sombrero

Look, I've been softening, not my poll numbers which are still great, despite what pollsters say, but about immigration. I don't want to hurt anyone. I want everyone to be great and am touched by thousands of people telling me they love me but it's not good to take families that've been here twenty years and just throw them out. That's too tough. I'm not talking about giving illegal aliens citizenship. I'm just saying let them pay taxes. That's not amnesty. That's working with them. I've been talking to Hispanic leaders. They see I'm a good guy. I smile and put on the sombrero they offer and dance, quite well I think, to the mariachi band celebrating our progress. Then I down several tamales. I love Mexican food.

What happens later that day and all the next? My Republican backers start calling me a flip flopper and a traitor as they shout: where's the wall? What about the mass deportations? Let me explain. There's no path to legalization unless the illegals leave the country. They have to leave and come back and start paying taxes. I know, many have been paying taxes for years but I don't talk about that. It's better to imply they've been freeloading. I'm really most concerned about bad dudes, the criminals, and there may be millions who I'll begin deporting the day I become president.

Will I then deport the law-abiding illegal aliens? I don't know but there's a good chance the answer could be yes. Let's see what happens. For now, I've put my new sombrero on the dresser because I'll probably need it again.

Calling for Hillary

By email I noncommittally volunteered to join a call squad for Hillary Clinton in northeast Bakersfield. An organizer phoned the night before to confirm my attendance, and about ten on Saturday morning I drove up the city's only hill to join a group of six eager Democrats waiting on the community patio in a gated community. Kern County is Republican territory where Congressman Kevin McCarthy, a native, usually gets about seventy percent of the vote and red presidential candidates seize almost as much. This meeting, I learned, wasn't focused on the impossible task of helping Hillary capture Kern; it was about calling battleground Nevada voters who, according to computer-generated programs, had voted for a Democrat at least once in recent elections.

We walked to the nearby home of the hostess and a brief training session began. A script would appear on laptop screens provided by volunteers, and they'd read or improvise when a click alerted them the computerized predictive dialer had eliminated dozens, perhaps hundreds of unanswered or busy phones – eighty percent generally are not answered – and a listener awaited. Rather than continue undercover, I confessed I was there to write an article, and gave my business card to the hostess, a Hispanic lady who noted that Donald Trump has galvanized more historically-apathetic Latino voters than any candidate she's seen.

"If you get a 'No,' that's the end of the conversation," said an experienced operative, a lady who'd driven up from Los Angeles that morning. "Whether or not they're backing Hillary, try to talk to them about Catherine Cortez Masto. She's running for Harry Reid's senate seat and was Nevada's attorney general."

Four volunteers joined me around the dining room table, one commandeered the couch, and another stationed herself at a desk in a bedroom. The presentations began and generally sounded about like this: "Hi, my name's Sally Jones, and I'm a volunteer for Hillary for

America. How are you doing? Good. Can we count on your support in the election on November eighth? Great. Do you have any interest in volunteering for the campaign? Okay. (Instructions were given to the few who said yes, and their names entered a database.) And please encourage your friends and family to vote for Hillary. Thank you."

The genial hostess offered roasted peanuts to those interested, and I was, despite my frenzied note-taking. We also sipped cold bottled water. Time moved swiftly. At the end of the two-hour session, after a young lady said, "I've got to hurry. I have a child," I read aloud several responses the callers had received and told us about, and asked for some others. Highlights follow:

1. My whole family is voting for Hillary.

2. We're voting for her but don't have time to volunteer.

3. What volunteer opportunities do you have?

4. I'm already a volunteer. Please take me off this list.

5. I'm not a supporter.

6. Take me off this damn list.

7. I don't like that bitch.

8. She's the wife of a bleep. (The volunteer declined to offer a specific profanity.)

9. Would you like to stay on the line and die?

Who do you suppose number nine's backing?

Calling for Trump

As required, I registered online for Kern County Trump Training and printed a free ticket necessary to enter the event. Downtown Bakersfield isn't Manhattan but can be a difficult place to park about six on a weeknight, and I had to cruise several minutes before finding the last spot on 19th Street, and then walked east past several eternally-empty commercial properties and turned left onto bustling Chester Avenue where I entered the front door of JC's Place, a modest but chandeliered ballroom advertised as available for receptions, parties, weddings, and quincianeras. A congenial lady, one of three people staffing the entrance table, scanned my ticket, asked me to sign in, and said, "Sit wherever you want."

I chose the only unoccupied table, in the rear, and estimated some fifty people were watching West Walker, a tall, suit-and-tie Donald Trump operative and teacher from near Los Angeles, point to a large video screen as he said, "There's a huge demand for Trump in California, not just among Republicans, also Democrats and independents and other groups. Our challenge is to reach those people. Let's see a show of hands. How many of you have never worked on a campaign?"

About ninety percent raised hands. Walker noted that's always the response in this campaign, new people looking for unique leadership.

"If there's a high turnout, Trump wins," he said. "You're the silent majority, Californians for Trump. We built our ground game so we were ready for the primary, and we need to do the same for the general election. We'll have strike teams go to Nevada, and we'll pay for your room and board. Some people will focus on specific targets. We're also using the social media, Facebook and Twitter. (Candidate Trump is a reflexive user of the latter.) The social media reaches some people who aren't touched by the traditional ground game. That's important because what the media says is often flat-out lies. You should look at the primary source documents."

I saw one black lady in attendance. It's impossible to be sure how many Latinos were present but I surmised not many if any. Most attendees were white and, just guessing, not beneficiaries of advanced education.

"How many of you are Democrats?" asked West Walker.

One lady smiled and raised her hand, then two other people admitted the affiliation.

Walker, augmented by a list on the screen, talked about many positions that need volunteers: office manager, coordinator, data manager, sign manager, Facebook manager. He added there are coalitions for veterans, African Americans, Latinos, farmers, and others. Team Trump also forms phone bank teams and voter registration drives.

"Don't wear a sports coat when canvassing neighborhoods," said Walker. "Dress one step up from those you expect to meet. It's better not to wear Trump clothes. Safety first. It's okay to wear a Trump pin on your lapel. Just knock on the doors and smile. Don't argue. And don't walk on the lawn. We want the power of personal visits. Ask if they'd like to have a Trump sign for their front yard.

"On voting day we'll bring our lists of known Trump supporters to the polling places and compare them to the updated lists, posted outside, of those who've voted."

"Can I use my Apple computer to make calls from home?" someone asked.

"You can use just about any computer but Apple. We're working on that."

Walker asked people to get in groups by zip code, exchange personal information, talk about ways they can set up call teams and local rallies, and to give three reasons why they want to vote for Donald Trump. My group included two other men and one woman.

After chatting a few minutes, I asked, "Why do you support Donald Trump?"

These reasons emerged: illegal immigration; Trump's not a career politician; he's not taking donations from large corporations; he knows how to make money, not waste it.

A stocky fellow added, "How can we elect a woman married to a guy who was impeached?"

"Bill Clinton was impeached, but he wasn't convicted," I said.

"Oh, I thought he was throwed out."

TWENTY-ONE

Trump Invades Mexico

I like that cute little guy, Enrique Peña Nieto, president of Mexico. He showed big balls by inviting me to visit him in Mexico City. The guy's smart, too. He knows I'm going to be the next president of the United States and wants to get ready to do some business. When I fly down in my Trump jet this morning, he treats me like I'm already in command. In our private meeting we talk about my wall on the border but we don't discuss who'll pay for it. That's for later. I'm here as a friend of Mexicans and want to shut off the guns and criminals that go from our country into theirs as well as the millions of criminal and freeloading Mexicans who illegally invade the United States every year. I'm confident we can work everything out.

After our great discussion, I'm honored to appear publicly with President Peña Nieto. We both give dignified speeches and look respectfully at the other as we speak. I don't even correct him when he says he told me Mexico won't pay for the wall. Like I said, that's for later. Right now we're building bridges, not walls.

This afternoon I fly home, to Arizona, feeling like the most powerful man on earth. Really, who else would it be? Certainly not Hillary Clinton. I'm not even thinking about her tonight in this hot border state. I'm telling tough and excited Americans we'll build a wall along the southern border, and Mexico will pay for the wall one-hundred percent. They'll be happy I've envisioned a beautiful and impenetrable wall enhanced by sensors above and below ground, so the aliens can't tunnel in, and guard towers and aerial surveillance. My supporters shout I'm the only one who can deliver security and greatness. I'm sure President Peña Nieto agrees.

Hidden Hillary

trump
snatches
votes
while
hidden
hillary
inhales
emails
and
money

A Text for You

During another difficult day of assisting Hillary Clinton in matters personal and political, Huma Abedin enters a private office, closes the door, and melts into a big soft chair where she digs a cell phone from her purse and begins to read text messages, the principal of which is from husband Anthony Weiner, a former congressman who's sent a photo of himself, resplendent in purple jockey shorts, and the note, "I want you back."

"You're out," she responds.

"We have so much."

"Had."

"I never touched those women."

"You wanted to and bragged about always being horny."

"That's biology. Can't help it."

"Other men can."

"Not Bill Clinton."

"Don't disrespect Hillary," she writes.

"He did a thousand times more, yet Hillary stayed."

"I'm not Hillary."

"I want to come home."

"Move on."

"This time I'll promote your political career."

"I don't want spotlight."

"You'd be wonderful, Huma Weiner, first female president."

"Hillary'll be first."

"Run against her as independent."

"Too late to register," Huma writes.

"With me guiding blitzkrieg campaign, you can win as write-in."

"You're fantasizing again."

"Please trust me."

"No."

"One more chance."

Tired of typing, Huma takes and sends a selfie of a young man kissing her neck.

Secret Trump

can't
tell
you
my
isis
plan
or
isis'll
know
too

Dr. Trump Assesses Hillary

I could've been a great doctor and am using that inherent talent when I tell you Hillary Clinton is a very sick woman. I'm not talking about her obvious emotional problems: lying, stealing, jeopardizing national security, and letting herself be abused by a serial skirt chaser. I'm talking about her physical health and, frankly, I'm quite worried. I know Hillary well. We used to socialize and be good friends. I often gave her money for campaigns and other political purposes, but now I'm afraid she's going to jail or worse.

Look what happened the other day in Manhattan. It wasn't hot, only about eighty-one in the shade. Hillary just sat inside with others to commemorate the fifteenth anniversary of the barbaric 9/11 attack on New York, but an hour and a half into the ceremony she said she was overheating and had to leave. Agents eased her into the SUV. I'd like to know her real medical problems and so would you. Later that day, after resting at her daughter's apartment, she looked weak and disoriented as she walked around outside, trying to convince people she's physically fit. Only a few days earlier she'd coughed her way through a speech. It's sad. She and her doctors claim it's only a case of pneumonia. Okay, release her medical records. You've seen the report from my doctor: I'm an extraordinary specimen. That's more important than the tax reports Democrats keep asking for.

I'm closing fast in the polls because Hillary spends so little time on the campaign trail. She's home resting. Why? What's wrong with her? She's a megalomaniac who'd do anything to become president, yet she can't work hard enough to promote herself. She's very weak and low energy and seems ready to faint. She's fallen a few times, too, and had blood clots in her brain, so we need to see medical evidence the clots really are gone. I don't care what her doctors say. This woman can't match my strength and vigor.

Trump's Physical Examination

Donald Trump and his large secret service detail enter Dr. Gilbert's office, and a nurse immediately escorts the candidate and two agents back to an examination room.

"I'm sorry, Mr. Trump, but Dr. Gilbert is ill," says the nurse.

"Why the hell didn't you tell me? I'm extremely busy."

"He just fainted a short while ago."

"Let's get outta here," says Trump.

"Don't worry… Dr. Johnson, a superb family practitioner next door, has agreed to step in and give you your annual physical examination."

"I want Dr. Gilbert."

"He's in an ambulance and we simply don't know when he'll be available. A man your age, under such stress, needs his physical now."

"All right. Tell Dr. Johnson I'll wait two minutes."

In about half that the doctor walks in and says, "Hello, Mr. Trump. I'm sure you've been told who I am. Please get undressed down to your underwear and put on this gown. I'll be back in five minutes."

Trump eyes the plump doctor who's about his age, wears heavy black glasses, and has long black hair. "Sorry, I don't do lady doctors."

"Naturally you're not going to do me, Mr. Trump. I'm going to do you. Please get undressed."

Dr. Johnson leaves, and Trump orders the agents and nurse to wait outside. Dr. Johnson returns, and Trump permits only the nurse, a young lady, to join them.

"I see you're rather heavy, Mr. Trump, perhaps thirty pounds overweight."

"I'm planning to lose fifteen. That's plenty."

"I understand you eat large portions of rich food."

"I'll cut back a little."

"Lean back on the table and let's give you an EKG."

Trump complies.

"Very good, Mr. Trump, healthy readings for a man of seventy."

"Good for a man any age."

"Perhaps not quite as good as when you were twenty. Now, please sit up and let me listen to your lungs. Hmmm. You ever smoke, Mr. Trump?"

"Not a puff in my life. Not a single drink, either. You hear something in my lungs?"

"Nothing catastrophic. Perhaps a touch of bronchitis or just an imperfection of aging."

"I'm not coughing, doctor."

"But you've surely coughed at some point in your life."

"Probably, but I can't remember when."

"How's your memory?"

"Like a brand new steel trap."

"Any family history of dementia."

"My father had Alzheimer's."

"That may be why you can't remember coughing."

"I remember but don't know when because it's been so damn long."

"Please stand, Mr. Trump, and pull down your underwear."

"I dunno. Only beautiful young women see me like this."

"I'm simply checking for testicular cancer, hernias, or other regional issues."

Trump's shorts fall to his ankles.

"Please turn your head to the right and cough. That's fine. All right, now turn to the left and cough. I think your testicles are fine, Mr. Trump. Now, please turn around, bend over, and place your elbows on the examination table."

Dr. Johnson gloves her right hand and proceeds until Trump screams, "Oh my god..."

The agents barge in, and one tackles Dr. Johnson, driving her onto the floor where her black glasses and wig fall off.

"Hillary," says Donald Trump.

Ohio and Florida

i'm worried the donald's now
up in ohio and florida says
a democrat

those polls don't matter
say several others at
meeting

why not

trump's hateful uninformed
and unelectable

but maybe hillary's hateful
shifty and unelectable

TWENTY-TWO

The First Debate

I don't care more than twenty million jobs were created when Bill Clinton was president. I'm telling the world during this first presidential debate that in the nineties Bill signed NAFTA, the worst trade deal anywhere, and Hillary was responsible. Excuse me, Hillary, I'm talking. Stand there and listen to me interrupt you. I'm a hundred pounds heavier and can kick your ass and get young tail anytime I want. All that helps me understand you're going to increase taxes and regulate companies out of business and keep piling regulations on top of regulations. And, I gotta grimace, you've been fighting ISIS your entire adult life but are still such a fool you use your website to tell our enemies how you'll beat them. General Douglas MacArthur wouldn't do that. I know because I'm a great warrior, at least I could've been.

You haven't accomplished anything, Hillary, and don't laugh I'm blaming you for everything. You are responsible. You've been in power thirty years and should know the Federal Reserve Bank is being used in a very political way. Fed chairwoman Janet Yellen, who isn't the kind of babe I date, is keeping interest rates low and propping up a weak stock market that will crash when Barack Obama leaves office and Yellen raises rates while Obama hides on golf courses the rest of his African life.

Quiet, Hillary. I'll explain, you listen. The only reason I'm not releasing my federal tax returns is because I'm undergoing an audit. When the audit's complete, I'll show everyone. You release your thirty-three thousand emails and I'll release my returns before the audit's complete.

I'm smiling for the cameras, Donald, but will kick your shins if you don't let me talk. The moderator, laid back Lester Holt, isn't being a proper referee. It doesn't matter. I've got the floor and like the rest of the American people suspect you're not as rich as you claim, and maybe not as charitable as you brag, and maybe you haven't paid any taxes at all, and I wonder who you owe money to and how much.

About those emails, I apologize for making a mistake.

The emails weren't a mistake, Hillary. That was done purposely. Many of your assistants have had to take the Fifth Amendment. That's disgraceful. It's about time this country has someone running it who understands money.

If your main claim to the presidency is business, you have some problems. I've met many people you've stiffed – carpenters, plumbers, electricians. You refused to pay thousands of people who labored for you, people who built your Trump monuments and made you wealthy. Do you really understand money? You've filed business bankruptcy six times. Sometimes there's not a direct transfer of ability from business to government.

Let's talk about race, shall we, said Lester Holt.

There are so many good police officers who want reform and to tackle the plague of gun violence.

That's weak, Hillary. You should get out more. Today I just got the endorsement of the Fraternal Order of Police and I'm so proud. They understand that four thousand people have been killed in Chicago, Obama's home city, since he became president. Thousands have been wounded there just this year. We must take away guns from bad people and use stop and frisk to establish law and order.

It's unfortunate Donald paints such a dire picture of the black community. They have churches and businesses and many wonderful activities. And don't you make fun of me for not spending more time in communities. I prepared for this debate, and I prepared to be president. You launched your political career on the racist birther charge that President Obama was born in Kenya.

I'm proud of that. I was the only one who could force him to finally show his birth certificate. You tried to do the same thing against him in the 2008 primaries. Oh yes you did. Besides, I've developed very good relations with the black community.

That's surprising, Donald. In 1973 you were sued by the Justice Department because you wouldn't rent apartments to blacks.

I was very young then, and a lot of people were sued. We settled that housing lawsuit without any admission of guilt. I must say, Hillary, that I recently watched your debates with Obama in 2008, and you treated him with terrible disrespect.

Let's discuss security, Lester Holt suggested.

Donald invited the Russians to hack into the computers of the Democratic National Committee. That's traitorous.

Really? Many admirals and generals are endorsing me, and ICE, too. This is the first time ICE has backed any presidential candidate. I'm very proud. They know who can defend this country. You and President Obama created a void in Iraq when you left. We should have left some troops, maybe ten thousand. We also should have taken the oil.

We couldn't work out a judicial agreement with Iraq about how to deal with American soldiers charged with crimes, Hillary said. That's why we left. Unlike you, who regularly insult Muslims all over the world, we're cooperating with them. We're also working with NATO, the most enduring military alliance in world history.

You and Obama saved Iran. They were collapsing under the sanctions until you signed the nuclear deal which is the most catastrophic ever. Regarding our NATO allies, I love them but they've got to start paying their fair share.

Don't accuse me of supporting the invasion of Iraq in 2003, Hillary. I knew it would destabilize the region and be a disaster. In 2002 I may have said something I can't remember on Howard Stern's radio show but after that I said invading was a bad idea. You, on the other hand, played the warmonger. I have much better judgment than you, and there's no question that I also have a better temperament.

You said Iranian soldiers who taunted U.S. servicemen should have been blown out of the water. That's not good judgment or temperament. You also have a cavalier attitude about nuclear weapons. You think it's okay for Japan and South Korea and others to develop doomsday weapons. A man who can be provoked by a tweet should not have his finger on the nuclear trigger.

That's an old one.

But a very good one, said Hillary.

You don't understand deals. China should take care of North Korea. They could easily do so. I'm still shocked by your Iran nuclear deal, one of the worst deals ever made by any country.

Unlike you, Donald, I am reassuring our allies we have mutual defense treaties and we will honor them. I understand real plans. You have no plan to defeat ISIS.

You don't have the heart to get deals done, Hillary. You need some basic ability and you have to be able to negotiate. You also need stamina, which I don't think you have.

As soon as you travel to a hundred twelve countries, as I did, then you can talk to me about stamina.

You have experience, but it's bad experience.

You have experience calling women pigs and slobs and hanging out at beauty contests.

You've spent hundreds of millions of dollars on negative ads against me, said Donald.

Will you both promise to support the outcome of this election, asked Lester Holt.

I will support the outcome, said Hillary.

Of course. I just want to make America great again.

Smooth Operator

i know more about
taxes than any
candidate ever
and am too smart
to pay learn my
secrets at trump
university

Putin Picks VP Winner

Ask my opponents in Russia and they'll tell you those who publicly insult me are sometimes shot or imprisoned. I thought about them as Tim Kaine frequently interrupted Mike Pence during the vice presidential debate. I realize Kaine, a smalltime apparatchik, may have been so nervous he hyperactively abandoned his polite demeanor to serve as Hillary Clinton's pit bull, and because of this I may not have disciplined Kaine, had I been his target. I simply would have privately told him he better behave.

I think Mike Pence, a more skilled debater and politician than Kaine, will be respectful when he serves as Donald Trump's vice president. Trump, as we know, has said I'm a better leader than President Obama so the challenger probably doesn't really agree with Pence's declaration the United States will bomb Syrian military targets to stop my bombers from destroying enemies of the Bashar al-Assad regime. How would bombing Assad's soldiers stop me from killing enemies of my ally? Pence was merely playing the hawk since Hillary's a hawk and Trump's a hawk but one who wants to be my friend and convince me to help the United States destroy ISIS.

I therefore also discount Mike Pence's statement that the Russian Bear never sleeps, he only hibernates. But after the campaign I'll have to tell President Trump that Pence is incorrect Hillary permitted the rise of an aggressive Russia. She couldn't have stopped my moderate moves to discipline our historical breadbasket, the Ukraine, and absorb our dear little brother, the Crimea. Pence also complained about my being close to the Iranians. I wouldn't say we're close but, unlike many in the United States and Israel, I'm not anxious to bomb them, either.

On these matters, at least, Mike Pence was correct: I don't respect Clinton and Obama and I do revere strength. That's why I'm so audacious as to spend eleven percent of what the United States devotes to defense. If Pence thinks that's excessive, after this campaign and its irrelevant rhetoric, I know The Donald and I can settle him down.

The Trump sons can help while I entertain Ivanka.

Trump Talk

sermonizers
pretend
they've
never
talked
trash
like
trump

Pussy Hound

Ladies, come on, please. Be honest. In that private conversation I was only pounding my chest to impress handsome young television host Billy Bush. Sure, I've often kissed beautiful women when I met them, but most seemed to like it. They sure didn't protest. That's what it's like when you're a star. Now, really, I'm going to have to get tough defending my boast about grabbing pussy. You know damn well I didn't mean that literally. But a lot of hypocritical people are making this a moral issue so I'll explain. I was just saying I got a lot of pussy. I always did. In prep school I was voted the class ladies' man. And over the years my wealth and fame and charisma made even more ladies want me. Look at the babes I've had. Don't pretend Bill Clinton is any different. Actually, he's way worse. It's shocking what he's told me out on the golf course. You tolerated anything from him. And one more thing. Tell us what you say when you're in private with other ladies. I doubt you'll do that right now. You're busy preaching. That's okay. Here's the truth: you talk about men the same way we talk about women.

Cesar Chavez Discusses Trump

Every year at least twice I drive to Keene, in the golden hills east of Bakersfield, to visit the Chavez National Monument and interview the proprietor, Cesar Chavez, founder of the United Farm Workers. Two days ago we met in his office, now housed in his museum. To maintain the feel of the sixties, the office still does not have a computer.

George Thomas Clark – Since you're not plugged in, I guess you haven't heard about Donald Trump's just-released remarks about grabbing women in delicate places.

Cesar Chavez – That's something I could've gotten from TV or radio, and besides in my private space I have all the high tech marvels. We were among the earliest users of computers to enhance our political and business networks, you know.

GTC – That's right. So what do you think?

CS – It's actually a relief. Even when Trump rallied in September, and led Hillary Clinton in some battleground states, I didn't think he could win. He's got too many enemies, many of them my people, the working people of color. Now, I know he can't win. How many women are going to vote for a guy like that? He's always been an egomaniac but he's becoming unhinged. Those three a.m. tweets to Alicia Machado, the former Miss Universe, were bizarre. It's frightening Trump believes Americans want a president who behaves like that.

GTC – Some analysts are saying Trump hasn't only ruined his presidential chances, he's destroyed the Trump brand.

CS – He's damaged the brand but I doubt he's destroyed it. He's a talented promoter and will probably always have a lot of money. However, if The Donald ever really is out on his ass, I guarantee we'll offer him a job in the fields.

GTC – That's very generous, Cesar, but Trump's seventy years old. He deserves some compassion.

CS – Absolutely. I wouldn't have him stooping and picking. He'd be hawking burritos in front of the lunch truck.

TWENTY-THREE

The Second Debate

I'm paying two grand for what feels like a ringside seat at the second Clinton-Trump debate and feel damn nervous before the two challengers come out and more tense when, surrounded by handlers, they march into the ring onstage. Former political champions and other celebrities aren't introduced beforehand. That's good. We want rhetorical violence now.

Trump ducks Hillary's hook and counters, Obamacare is a disaster, the Iran nuclear deal is one-sided, our trade deficit's eight-hundred-billion dollars, and two more police were killed today. We shouldn't be worried about my locker room talk. I'm not proud of it but didn't at all say I sexually assaulted anyone. In a world of ISIS, there are more important issues. I'll knock hell out of ISIS, by the way.

The video represents exactly who Donald is, Hillary jabs. He rates and insults women. He's targeted Muslims and immigrants and many others. He doesn't understand we're great because we're good.

Bill Clinton did far worse than anything I ever did. He was abusive. He's by far the worst in our presidential history. He was impeached and fined eight-hundred-fifty-thousand dollars in civil court. Four of his victims, who Hillary attacked viciously, are here tonight.

This man never apologizes for anything, says Hillary. He's insulted the Muslim father of an American war hero. He spread the racist lie that President Obama wasn't born in the United States. He said a distinguished federal judge wasn't qualified to rule on immigration since his parents were born in Mexico. He owes all of them an apology.

You owe President Obama an apology, Trump says. You sent around those pictures of him in African garb. You should be apologizing for that and the thirty-three thousand emails you deleted. There've never been so many lies. If I win I'll assign a special prosecutor to look into this. It's a disgrace.

We're so fortunate we don't have someone like Donald Trump in in charge of this country.

Because you'd be in jail.

I'm very sorry about those emails. I used bad judgment, but there's no evidence my server was hacked. No classified information was lost.

And yet, Hillary didn't even know what the letter C stood for on the documents.

Hillary shakes her head and says, this is the big diversion to try to keep people from thinking about your exploding campaign and the way so many Republicans are deserting you. I'm interested in the issues. You say Obamacare's a disaster. I respond that ninety percent health care coverage is best in our history. Costs are going up but I want to fix the system, not destroy it.

Bernie Sanders said Hillary has very bad judgment. I have wonderful judgment. That's why I understand Muslims have to report when they see something. In San Bernardino people saw bombs and guns at the young couple's house. Hillary can't even call it what it is: radical Islamic terrorism.

We need American Muslims to be part of our eyes and ears, she says. They want to feel welcome in this country.

I welcome Muslims after extreme vetting in Syria and other places. People are coming into our country and we don't know who they are or how they feel about us.

We are a country founded on religious freedom and liberty. The things Donald says are recruiting tools for ISIS.

We're letting people in this country who are going to commit crimes. Hillary wants everyone to just come right in. She has bad judgment and should never be president.

I know the American people are confident I can be president but they're afraid of Donald because his friends the Russians have been hacking into our computers. We need to study his tax returns to see if there are any dangerous entanglements.

I think it would be great if we got along with Russia. Taxes – I pay hundreds of millions of dollars in taxes. Hillary's friends Warren Buffett and George Soros have the same deductions, and they've given her millions so she can buy far more TV ads than I have. She wants to raise taxes even though our country has low growth, no growth.

Donald lives in an alternative reality. He hasn't paid federal taxes in twenty years. He wants to cut taxes for the wealthy and raise taxes on the middle class. I want to invest in you. Since the Republican-induced recession, all money has gone to the top.

I understand the tax code better than anyone who has ever run for president. Of course I've used the same deductions as Buffett and Soros. I pay state taxes, real estate taxes, sales taxes. Since Hillary doesn't like the tax code, why didn't she change when she was a senator?

Because there was a Republican president.

Because she was an ineffective senator.

Let's talk about Syria and President Assad, Hillary says. The Russian air force is bombing Aleppo and killing thousands of civilians. The Russians don't care about ISIS. They want Trump as president.

She talks tough against Syria but she's weak, like Obama. When he drew a line in the sand there, the whole world laughed. I don't like Assad but we have to crush ISIS, and he's killing ISIS and so are the Russians and Iran. By the way, that Iran nuclear deal was a catastrophe. I understand these dangers and that's why so many generals and admirals have endorsed me and twenty-one Congressional Medal of Honor winners. From heaven General Patton also supports me.

General Patton would prefer me as a commander to Donald, Hillary says. I'd target ISIS leader Baghdadi and arm the Kurds and Turkish fighters in and near Syria. I have real military strategies.

I'd like to assure blacks and other minorities that I can be president of all the people. But Hillary can't. She said half my supporters belong in a basket of deplorables. She isn't going to do anything for blacks. Our inner cities are a disaster. She's all talk.

Sixty-seven percent of the people in New York voted to reelect me, and I'm very proud and humbled. Many of them and people throughout the country are worried there wouldn't be a place for them in Donald Trump's America. I can unite people despite what I said about Donald's supporters. My problem isn't really with his supporters. My problem is with him.

Hillary has tremendous hate in her heart. My heart is open even at three a.m. when I tweet about a hefty Miss Universe from twenty years ago. Twitter and Facebook are very effective means of communication.

In contrast to my opponent, I want a Supreme Court that will stick with Roe v. Wade and equality in marriage. Donald would bring in people to overturn liberty.

Judge Antonin Scalia died and we have a vacancy, he says. I'm looking for judges in the mold of Scalia, people who would respect the Constitution of the United States. I can't be influenced by outsiders. Nobody can push me. I've put a hundred million dollars of my own money into my campaign. Hillary has made two hundred fifty million. Why doesn't she at least put thirty million of her money into her campaign so there would be thirty million less for special interests forcing her to do what they want? They're killing our energy companies. The Environmental Protection Agency is so restrictive.

Despite people like Donald, we are energy independent.

A spectator stands and shouts, can either of you name one positive thing that you respect in one another.

I don't agree with most anything Donald says, but I respect his wonderful family.

I will say this about Hillary Clinton. She's a fighter, she's not a quitter.

Obama Seeks Third Term

Folks, did you watch that debate the other night? Goodness gracious this great nation ought to offer two candidates better than those we saw on that town hall stage. Now, you know I'm an ally of Hillary Clinton and have often praised her work as my secretary of state, and I maintain that position. She was an able aide. But she doesn't have my dynamism, wisdom, or wit. She's rather a plodding bureaucrat. And Donald Trump's a charlatan I expect to soon show up wearing white sheets. He ought to add a dunce cap to his uniform for I have never seen a presidential candidate remotely as ignorant of issues as The Donald. He may not understand public policy but at least he long knew I was born in Kenya until he ceased knowing it.

You realize I'm right about these two and the dreary candidates they beat in the primaries. Terror is loose in our cities as well as in Syria and Iraq and Russia and Ukraine and Asia and many other troubled regions, and we know who can best deal with problems foreign and domestic. Indeed, he's the very man in the White House today, Barack Hussein Obama. I say this not in a self-promotional way but as a patriot ready to sacrifice daily golf and frequent corporate speeches by continuing to serve you, the freedom-loving American people.

But you've already served the maximum two four-four terms, some will say.

That is true but not an insuperable obstacle. We have merely to revise the Twenty-Second Amendment, passed in the aftermath of four-term Franklin Roosevelt, that currently restricts even a president of rare talent and temperament. But do we really want to remove a virtuoso and replace him with a dunce? We certainly wouldn't do that in private business, and should not do so in the business of state.

In that regard I propose, in fact I order, the Congress of the United States to convene this very afternoon for the purpose of voting on and passing an addendum to the Twenty-Second Amendment stating that in critical times a commander in chief may continue his office as long as the free and thoroughly-informed American people shall elect him. I'm confident that by late this evening I'll have the necessary Constitutional mandate and at that time will address the nation, and indeed the world, to announce the blessed news that I intend to run for a third term as your president.

As a stable and realistic man I acknowledge that even I probably could not overcome the divided Democratic, and non-deplorable, vote if Hillary stayed in the race. If she'd had to face me in the 2016 presidential primary, I would have trounced her. I erred in not moving to change the Twenty-Second Amendment months ago. I must therefore persuade Hillary not to drop out of the race but to run as my vice presidential mate. If she refuses, what will I do? I'll first portray her as a woman determined to deliver our highest office into the small and ignoble hands of a beast. If that move proves insufficient, I'll reveal troubling tapes of Hillary browbeating and threatening the paramours of her husband, the lascivious and utterly uncontrollable Bill Clinton, who should never again be allowed to live in and besmirch the sacred chambers of our White House. If even that is unsuccessful, I will be compelled to arrest Hillary for treason because of her likely-tragic security lapses regarding tens of thousands of sensitive, and often classified, State Department emails.

That would leave The Donald head to head with me. And even the Republicans know I'd tear him several new assholes.

Presidential Behavior

(Donald Trump and Bill Clinton met this afternoon in a Manhattan dungeon where a supposedly-private debate was deviously recorded by the KGB, which minutes ago released this voice-verified tape.)

Donald Trump – Bill, you're a disgraceful pervert and, like your wife, should be in jail.

Bill Clinton – My wife's not a pervert.

DT – She's a secret-leaking liar who's put our country in great danger.

BC – If anyone should be behind bars, Donald, it's you, and not just for tax evasion and stiffing your construction workers and bilking students of Trump University, but because of your outrageous mistreatment of women.

DT – No one in political history has degraded and abused women like you. I'm surprised you'd even bring up the subject.

BC – That's what we're here to debate.

DT – And that's more amazing still. Let's start with Juanita Broaddrick, who you raped after luring her into a Little Rock hotel room more than thirty years ago.

BC – I did not rape that woman, Ms. Broaddrick. What evidence do you have? Did she call the police? There's no evidence at all.

DT – She told some friends about it right afterward, and her husband at the time later said he saw where you'd bitten her lip.

BC – For your information, that same husband even later said he didn't remember seeing her bitten lip. Besides, another lady, who admits to having consensual sex with me, has also stated I bit her lip.

DT – Disgusting.

BC – I've at least entertained ladies in private. Jessica Leeds said that thirty-five years ago she was sitting in coach on an airplane and the stewardess offered a seat in first class that she accepted. Tragically, that seat was next to yours, and after asking if she was married you lifted the armrest and groped her breasts and tried to shove your hands up her skirt. According to the *New York Times*, she said she escaped from the "octopus" and ran to the rear of the plane.

DT – You mean according to the *Democratic Party's Times*. Hillary only has one thing going for her in this election, and that's the press.

BC – It looks like she's also got a lot more votes than you.

DT – Only because the press and liberal media don't emphasize how you abused Paula Jones twenty-five years ago. It's painful. You dropped your drawers and exposed yourself to the young lady.

BC – I did not. That's just what she says. She made a pass at me, but I declined because of my respect for Hillary. Paula Jones was a woman scorned.

DT – Then why did you and your attorneys agree to pay her eight-hundred-fifty grand.

BC – I sacrificed the money to stop a farcical distraction. I needed to concentrate on the economy and foreign policy, two areas about which you're quite ignorant. I keep up with all policy developments including how Rachel Crooks recently said in 2005 you met her outside an elevator in Trump Tower and shook hands but wouldn't let go and kissed her right on the mouth. Temple Taggart also said you kissed her on the lips more than once when she was under your control as a beauty contestant.

DT – I guarantee those ladies wanted me to kiss them and I probably would have if I hadn't been so busy. Their accusations are lies and pure wishful thinking.

BC – They're not all lying about you.

DT – Nor about you. I gotta say politics is even nastier business than construction or gambling.

BC – At least you'll be out of politics next month. I've got at least four more years.

Trump Apocalypse

I'm trying to save the nation not destroy it. Can't you see, as my passionate supporters do, it's Hillary Clinton who wants to ruin us all? She should've been in jail years ago. It's my destiny to put her there. She's spread our national secrets through a leaky email server, betrayed our now-dead diplomats in Benghazi, harassed and threatened the sexual victims of depraved Bill Clinton, and, most upsetting, there's a helluva lot of cellulite on her thighs.

This woman must not become commander in chief. Only I am qualified, as no rational person can deny after studying my overwhelming achievements in boardrooms, barrooms, bedrooms, and bankruptcy courts. Be honest. You think Hillary's had as many young men as I've had young women? You know she hasn't.

The liberal media is conspiring to confuse the voters and convince them I'm unfit to be president. I doubt that devious plan will work. But if it does, I can't guarantee what would happen.

No Concession

I was so close. Screw that. I am close. Look at this final debate. I'm on the verge of becoming president of the United States and leader of a movement to save the nation from terrorists, alien invaders, and greedy politicians. And crooked Hillary Clinton is the worst, a liar, a thief, and very nasty woman. I can't imagine the American people choosing a dumpy old wretch like that over a dynamic stud like me. Really. Can you? It's not fair. It's not fair at all. I can make this country great again, and I'm the only one bold and smart enough to do so. It's mandatory I become President Trump. I'm positive the majority of voters want me. But they're about to be disenfranchised. You know it. This election is rigged. Millions of people have registered to vote who shouldn't be registered. Hillary shouldn't even be allowed to run or vote. She's a felon who belongs in jail. I'm not going to answer loaded questions from the biased media about whether I'll accept the result of the election. I'll look at it at the time. That means I'll accept the results if I win because there's no way I can lose a fair election. If it isn't fair, maybe I won't accept the results. Why should I encourage the thieves by telling them they can get away with stealing the election? They better not try. You've seen my supporters.

GOP Genius

scholarly bakersfield
republican assaults
sikh for being muslim
terrorist while across
nation seventy percent
armed trumpsters vow
to reject clinton victory

Righteous Litigation

the donald
declares
all female
accusers
liars and
vows to sue
after election
and audit

March for America

Excitedly I open an email inviting me to March for America. I love invitations and scroll to learn more. I'll need to be at the golden-domed capitol in Sacramento on October twenty-ninth and thirtieth so I can be one of the "American citizens peacefully marching" here and near other capitols across the land. At noon we'll have a prayer for Mr. Trump and rededicate ourselves to "take back America, demand justice against government corruption, stop rigged elections, (and) demand the indictment of Hillary Clinton/ Bill Clinton and the Clinton Foundation."

The email doesn't say what we'll do next but logically I guess it would be to insist Donald Trump be indicted for abusing women and bilking his students. Maybe Hillary, Bill, and The Donald should be placed in a work-release program, toiling by day in the Oval Office and returning at night to a minimum security facility.

TWENTY-FOUR

Comey to the Rescue

i'm james comey
quite tall republican
director of fbi
and hope you know
i'm writing congress about
more hillary clinton emails
not so much hers but from
aide huma abedin's estranged
husband anthony weiner
who sexts lots of females
even minors and as
election nears maybe
this'll help americans
vote correctly

Anthony Weiner Counterattacks

I'm sick of people calling me a pervert and sicko and a disgrace. I am not. I'm just compelled to text women images of my underwear-clad self. Is that really bad? I didn't even commit adultery. I should be complimented for restraint. I've got a hard on several hours a day. You can't imagine how horny I am. Actually, whether you're man or woman I know most of you personally understand what I mean. Don't deny it. Oh, I know you'll deny it publicly. But don't bother lying to me. You're not much different except I acknowledge most of you wouldn't have texted a girl of fifteen. About that I am very sorry and not solely because I may be prosecuted. Maybe I didn't know how old she was. Did you consider that?

I'm not here to adjudicate my case but to blast my hypocritical enemies, starting with Donald Trump. Without photos I'm texting him this: #Pussy Grabbing political #Nincompoop ready to nuke world and rob poor if you become president.

To FBI director and Republican kingmaker James Coney I say: #Keep your #Lying face out of my computer, my wife's life, and the presidential election.

To Hillary Clinton I wistfully note: #Presidency was yours before you started acting half as dumb as #Weiner.

To Bill Clinton: #Bubba drop to your knees and thank #God there were fewer technological temptations in your day.

To my lovely but estranged wife Huma Abedin: #Keep pretending we #Don't know how your emails got on my desktop.

To the voters of America: #Your choice, Crooked but #Competent Hillary or a #Maniac.

The Klan's President

i've
got
few
newspaper
endorsements
but
one's
the
kkk
who i condemn
for being similar
to me

Trump Phones

just received this urgent email
trump phones
in kern county
need volunteers
today
to call from
kern to reach
battleground
state voters

wonder why team hillary
isn't sending
same message
now

Trump Math

Who wrote that headline? This isn't Trump math. This is scientific composite polling daily presented by *Real Clear Politics* and others who've acknowledged the facts and concluded I'm poised to become president of the United States.

I'm sure in private even Hillary Clinton isn't denying her doom. She knows, and it's painful for me to admit, that she had one of my balls in each hand and was ready to squeeze when James Comey finally grew a pair and alerted Congress and the nation he had scores of thousands of new emails involving Hillary's criminal behavior and breaches of national security. Comay didn't admit he'd read some of the emails and knew they weren't duplicates, but you know he must have verified wrongdoing or wouldn't have spoken so soon before the election. It's not like I've ever given the guy any money. But I'll sure let him remain in J. Edgar Hoover's office when I'm president.

My victory is almost inevitable. I'm still ahead in all the states I'd been leading, and in the four key battleground states where I'd trailed – Ohio, Florida, North Carolina, and Nevada – I've now surged into leads of one to three points. Big mo' is definitely named Donald, and a majority of Americans are finally through with the scandal-infested Clintons. All I've got to do in five days is win Colorado or Wisconsin or Pennsylvania or New Hampshire. Sure, the pollsters are trying to convince you I'm behind by two to five points in those states but you know any poll calling me a loser is rigged.

Frankly, I'm not only going to win next week, I'm going to win by a landslide. The FBI has teams of analysts reading those new emails around the clock and I'm sure there'll be an election-eve bombshell about Hillary heading to jail. What could save her? I doubt any more women are going to step forward and lie I groped them. They know they'll be sued just like those who've already lied.

TWENTY-FIVE

The Fuehrer Endorses Trump

I'm confident you know who I've always planned to endorse for president of the United States and have only delayed this official announcement to maximize the effect of my support. There is but one candidate, an American man of steel, who understands the most important of issues: your nation must be cleansed by deporting millions of racially-impure aliens. I support Donald Trump in his essential task of making America white again, and I've offered him not merely my racial and logistical expertise but that of Heinrich Himmler, my esteemed Reichsfuehrer SS, who discussed this matter with Trump last year.

Let the roundup begin. And build the wall as soon as possible. In candor, I must warn that Trump should use deportation and the wall as mere starting points. What he must really do, and quite soon, is engineer an Anschluss with Mexico and Canada, that is he needs to annex those countries to create more living space and defensible borders. I trust the implications are clear for those south of the border.

Donald Trump is correct that the United States must be prepared to restrain China and North Korea. Let me emphasize, however, that not even I would be so rash as to invade a nuclear nation of more than a billion people several thousand miles away. At least Trump will command a huge country wielding a vast navy – unlike my tiny Kriegsmarine – and can strangle and otherwise control the shipping lanes of the South China Sea. This will inevitably be quite dangerous but leaders who cringe and avoid risks are cowards unworthy of command. The risks can be minimized, as Trump has in a related way suggested, by encouraging and helping South Korea and Japan to become nuclear nations and aim their missiles at the Chinese, who are essentially Bolshevist Asians. And regarding communists, don't worry, I believe Trump won't actually embrace Vladimir Putin, either literally or figuratively, since the Russians are forever as dangerous as they are deceitful. He just wants to use the Russians economically, as I did after forging the Friendship Pact in 1939 and two years later watching Russian trains, laden with supplies for us, roll toward Germany as my soldiers, panzers, and planes attacked the Soviet colossus.

As in so many essential matters, I agree with Trump that America must resume waterboarding. Torture is often beneficial and should always be applied when enemies swallow information. The Donald, if I may be so informal, is also correct that waterboarding is rather lighthearted stuff compared to other measures he plans to use, and to the really quite grim techniques applied by the Gestapo. For a long time our adversaries were most reluctant to risk late-night knocks on their doors.

In a most personal way I understand Donald Trump's plan to sue women who lied that he sexually abused them. I faced similar charges, not from my tragic niece Geli Raubaul, who was dead by suicide, but from my political and media enemies who stated and printed the most outrageous lies about my relationship with Geli, who resided in my Munich apartment in 1931. I at all times behaved as a respectful uncle and did not, as jackals asserted, forbid her to socialize with men and did not quarrel loudly with her on the day of her death. A year and a half later, once I became chancellor, and soon thereafter Der Fueher, only masochists said unkind things about me or my beloved Geli. Trump will have a much more difficult task in controlling the American media, but even in your permissive time he should be able to bribe, intimidate, and sue most of his public enemies into relative restraint.

I so much resent those who have denounced Donald Trump for mimicking a disabled reporter and the incomprehensible English accents of Asians and others. If we'd had social media in my era, you'd today enjoy on YouTube my wonderful cutting impersonations of the lame, the dim, and the unfortunate. That's what powerful men do. They get stronger by making the weak weaker.

Trump is entirely justified in worrying about voter fraud, particularly as it would mean Hillary Clinton, female and corrupt, becomes president. His millions of nonwhite adversaries have no reason to behave honorably at the polls. In fact they're emboldened by the current Negro president to take power in whatever way they can. Please note, however, I tweeted Trump he should respect the outcome of any reasonably fair election, as I twice did in 1930 after losing to senile President von Hindenburg. Trump threatens a coup if he loses, but in America that's a fantasy. On November eighth he must win, for he won't later have my opportunity to enter government as chancellor.

Campaign Strategist

helpful
fbi
director
comey
announces
hillary's
emails
okay
after
all

Foxy News

on monday fox
news reports
the donald has
narrow but
expanding path
to electoral
victory does
fox believe
what it reports

Election Morning

trump pence email
need quarter million
californians to
call battleground
states

meanwhile obama
writes you should
already be phoning
and knocking on
doors for hillary

Election Watch

Sometimes I feel I shouldn't have married a Republican and was especially displeased when she refused to go to the election watch party, saying, "They're your friends and all Demos."

"Fine, then let's visit some of your conservative chums."

"This election's too important for socializing. Go on alone if you want."

I decided not to try that one, and turned on our huge flat screen bolted to the living room wall. My wife sat on the sofa and I in my adjacent reading chair.

"You better sedate yourself with a few drinks," I said. "And I'll have some so I don't feel too much of your pain seeing Trump slaughtered."

I got out the gold tequila, surmising The Donald wouldn't touch this Mexican brew even if he drank, and added orange juice and grenadine to one shot each, and my wife and I sipped in our usual moderate way. We do have much in common, especially reading, watching movies, and avoiding commercial TV, the latter preference prompting us to reject massive cable packages and select PBS for news. Tonight we'd also hop around the networks, avoiding commercials.

A large red and blue map of the United States appeared next to an electoral scoreboard.

"Your girl isn't doing too well," she said.

"She's doing fine."

Some veteran print journalists, TV correspondents, and political strategists said they weren't sure why Hillary wasn't faring better and someone surmised Trump must be getting hordes of white voters boosted by disenchanted citizens who hadn't visited the polls in a long time. I picked up a piece of paper on which I had the projections of recent battleground polls.

"No problem, at least for Hillary," I said. "You know she's going to take Trump in Pennsylvania, which hasn't gone presidential GOP since papa Bush in 1988, and she'll trounce him in Michigan and

Wisconsin."

"He'll defeat her in Ohio, as you know and your beloved polls have been indicating."

"Hold it. Donald Trump is Mr. Polls, unless they say he's losing, and then they're bogus."

"He's winning."

"For the moment," I said, writing on another paper the Clinton-Trump Electoral delegate count: 104-129 at about 6:30 p.m. in California.

I was getting us another round when I heard a pundit say, "Hillary's only performing like an average Democrat with blacks and Hispanics. It's not as overwhelming as she hoped. Only 80 percent of black men are voting for her."

"I hope those other 20 percent aren't voting for David Duke," I said, and at 6:37 wrote 104-137. "Tighter than expected in the Rust Belt."

"Than you and the Democrats expected. Those people have lost their jobs and homes and their dignity. Donald Trump wants to rebuild their lives."

"He wants to keep tapping into their anger. He doesn't really care about them. What has he ever done, other than boast during this campaign, to indicate he gives a damn about working people? He's always insulated himself behind gold-plated walls."

At 7:06 I wrote 109-150 and at 7:20, as Trump took Ohio, I noted 122-168, and a few minutes later, when Clinton won Virginia, I said, "We're gonna be up late. No point writing the times anymore."

I was into the presidential race, not the identity of every man and woman on PBS and the commercial networks, so to one of them goes credit for emphasizing that in Michigan non-college whites were voting 61-31 for Trump.

"No real surprise," I said, heading for the bar. "He's a long way from 270 Electoral votes."

"Easy on your sedation."

"You'll be needing it soon," I said, dreamily.

In about twenty minutes my wife, who I find quite lovely even when not buzzed, said, "I better do the bartending. You just relax and look at the screen." Clinton had lost Florida and trailed 131-197.

"After weeks of hearing about how few Electoral paths Trump had to victory, I'm glad the experts, who are quite liberal – maybe we do need FOX News – at least now admit Hillary's the one whose paths are closing."

"Trump's leading by 12 points with men and Clinton's leading with women by 12," said a guru.

"Women should be against Trump more than that," I said. "The man's a Neanderthal. As a woman, you should appreciate that."

"I'd rather spend the night with him than Hillary."

"I beg your pardon."

"I meant socially. You know I'm not attracted to flabby guys or men my dad's age."

"Aha, there's California and Washington for Hillary," I said. "She leads 202-201."

"That's irrelevant because it's been known for years. Look, there's North Carolina for The Donald. Write that down: 202-216."

Less than a drink later she said, "There's Iowa, 209-228."

It doesn't matter what time Trump won Pennsylvania to make it 215-264. "This isn't real. Donald J. Trump can't be president of the United States."

"You're in denial."

I still kept writing, 218-266, 218-269, and then those Wisconsin Badgers voted Trump, and I exhaled, "It's over. He didn't even need Michigan."

"But he'll get that, too."

"Let's go to bed."

"Grope me on the sofa first."

President-elect Trump

I've been saying I know how to win and meant it and now you see why as I lead my big happy family on stage to thank Hillary Clinton for years of public service and to urge the nation to bind its wounds and come together because I pledge to be president of all Americans. This isn't a campaign but an incredible and great movement. People of all races, backgrounds, and religions are joining me in the urgent task of rebuilding the nation and our infrastructure. We have tremendous potential in this time of national growth and renewal that enables us to dream of big, bold, beautiful things. We can do this in peace, for we will get along with all nations who wish to get along with the United States.

Trump Visits Obama

Less than two days after the polls closed President-elect Donald Trump escorts his bride Melania to the White House to visit President Barack Obama and his wife Michelle. Reports by the principals indicate all four interact amicably, ladies in the private living area and gentlemen in the Oval Office. There are no witnesses or films, and presumably no recordings, of the executive meeting, and we don't need them. We care not what the stiffly-polite men say but what they're thinking.

Barack Obama – Sit your fat ass down in my Oval Office I can't believe you'll soon be occupying.

Donald Trump – Enjoy the end of your disastrous eight years in a place you should've never been. I'll bring victory to this office.

BO – What was that birther nonsense all about?

DT – I enjoyed irritating you especially since you could've stopped the whole thing by simply providing your birth certificate.

BO – That was the real start of your presidential campaign. It made people notice you, but in a very negative way.

DT – You don't understand this nation or that I've won an overwhelming mandate.

BO – Donald, you lost the popular vote.

DT – But I won the Electoral College.

BO – The Electoral College is a farce.

DT – I agree, very undemocratic.

BO – We don't agree on much.

DT – At least we both know that during your time in office Democrats have been losing seats in the Senate and House of Representatives as well as in state legislatures. You're also losing governors.

BO – An election cycle that'll reverse after two years of your mishandling of the presidency.

DT – You still don't hear the people who want change.

BO – I hear them. Now please hear this: I guarantee you aren't going to deport eleven million undocumented people living and working in this country. You don't have the logistical resources and damn sure don't have a mandate for that. That's not what America is.

DT – I'm only starting with a couple million illegal aliens who're in jail here or criminals on the loose. We're going to round up those people and send them back where they came from. Your weak immigration policies have endangered and weakened this country.

BO – Since you read damn little you don't know I'm called the Deporter in Chief and have sent home more undocumented people than all presidents combined for more than a century. Reagan and both Bushes were weaklings compared to me.

DT – And what you did, though not entirely bad, was still not enough. You should've built a wall.

BO – We've got some walls and fenced areas I've increased.

DT – We don't have a real wall, and I'm going to build it and the majority of Americans will back me.

BO – The Mexicans aren't going to pay for your wall.

DT – It's not my wall, it's our wall. And they'll pay through tariffs and impounded remittances if they refuse to pay straight up.

BO – If you start trade wars with Mexico and China you'll set off an economic catastrophe.

DT – I'm going to create vast markets for American products.

BO – If you destroy economies in other countries, by denying them exports to the United States, they won't be able to buy much.

DT – You don't understand markets and business because you've been in academia and politics all your life.

BO – I know my Affordable Care Act enables more people, and a higher percentage, to have health insurance than at any time in our history.

DT – And millions still aren't insured because they can't afford the premiums. There's too much inefficiency.

BO – Don't try to repeal the ACA or you'll put millions of Americans at risk.

DT – I'm not saying Obamacare doesn't have any good features. I like it that insurance companies can't deny coverage because of pre-existing conditions and that kids at home, even up to age twenty-five, can stay on their parents' policies. I'll keep what's helpful and get rid of the rest.

BO – Be very careful how you deal with the Iranians. You're wrong that the nuclear deal is the worst ever. Without it, the Iranians would already have a weapon of mass destruction.

DT – You can't verify they aren't hiding something.

BO – We're as sure as we can be. That's what inspections are about.

DT – The inspections aren't tough enough or often enough and leave the Iranians too many opportunities to hide weapons.

BO – If you bomb them, they'll strike at America and American interests all over the world.

DT – I'll destroy them.

BO – Is that what you want?

DT – Maybe a preemptive strike, with Israel's help.

BO – Israel wants the United States to do the job.

DT – We're the only ones big enough.

BO – No one's big enough to prevent terroristic attacks.

DT – You mean Islamic terrorism.

BO – If that name pleases you and your backers. What I'm explaining is we can't keep bombing and drone-striking people and expect them to take it. They're going to hit back.

DT – I'll strike first and keep striking. There won't be any 9/11's or Pearl Harbors when I'm president.

BO – You've many times accused Hillary and me of creating ISIS. That's beyond specious.

DT – You destabilized the region by withdrawing U.S. troops from Iraq. That void was filled by ISIS.

BO – We withdrew because the Iraqis insisted on judicial control of U.S. soldiers in Iraq.

DT – I would've stayed and told them to shove it.

BO – The United States' illegal invasion was called Operation Iraqi Freedom. We can't destroy and occupy a country, supposedly to free it, and then reject its demands for judicial control of its territory.

DT – You're a failure.

BO – You're a hyperactive blowhard who'll lead us to disaster.

DT – Save the doomsday talk for your liberal friends. I'm going to give the nation what it wants, strong leadership and a true conservative Supreme Court.

BO – You spent much of your life as a liberal.

DT – Ronald Reagan was a liberal before he matured and became conservative. I've also matured. When I take office, I'm nominating a judge who's pro-life.

BO – So you can overturn Roe v. Wade.

DT – That should be the result.

BO – In addition to being ethically wrong, you'll lose the support of women.

DT – I've been hearing how much women hate me this whole campaign.

BO – Plenty do. And more will. You won't be reelected.

DT – Doesn't matter. I'll do what I've been promising, except for the improvised concessions of a born dealmaker.

BO – That knock means the ladies have finished their tour and are waiting.

DT – Can we invite them in?

BO – Absolutely.

Sources

"Ben Carson's Greatest Operation" – "Psychopaths' Brains Show Differences in Structure and Function," School of Medicine and Health, University of Madison-Wisconsin, November 22, 2011.

About the Author

George Thomas Clark is the author of *Hitler Here, The Bold Investor, King Donald, In Other Hands, Death in the Ring, Paint it Blue, Obama on Edge, Echoes from Saddam Hussein, and Tales of Romance.* He has also taught English as a Second Language for adults, published a monthly tabloid of features and columns, and been a material handler, salesman, and newspaper correspondent.

In addition to writing, Clark follows the news and sports, exercises daily (albeit delicately), collects contemporary art, enjoys independent movies, and travels to places (most recently Madrid, Mexico City, Quito, Guanajuato, and Aguascalientes) where he can socialize in Spanish.

The author's website is <u>GeorgeThomasClark.com</u>